CULTURE WINS

The Roadmap to an Irresistible Workplace

WILLIAM VANDERBLOEMEN

A SAVIO REPUBLIC BOOK
An Imprint of Post Hill Press
ISBN: 978-1-64293-807-4

Culture Wins
The Roadmap to an Irresistible Workplace
© 2020 by William Vanderbloemen
All Rights Reserved

posthillpress.com
New York • Nashville
Published in the United States of America

CONTENTS

ACKNOWLEDGMENTS

GREATNESS IS USUALLY FOUND within a person because another calls it out of them. I wouldn't know any success, we wouldn't have won any awards, and our business wouldn't be here without the steady guidance and counsel of my wife. Throughout the journey that Vanderbloemen has been, she has been the one calling greatness out of me that I didn't know was there. Thank you, Adrienne, for all you have done and are doing. And here's to continuing on this path and seeing what adventure awaits.

The Power of Culture

THIS BOOK WAS AN accident.

Team culture is usually an accident, but it doesn't have to be. Over the years, I've learned that there is a path to a winning culture, and it's a path that creates an irresistible workplace and a winning business.

Culture trumps your business idea. Culture trumps your strategic plan. Culture even trumps the competency of your team.

Culture wins—but it doesn't have to be accidental.

While this book was an accident, the cover design was not. The pathway to a winning culture is pretty much summed up by what looks like a random cover design.

Why in the world would anyone put a quirky orange circle on the cover of a book? Isn't this a book about culture and how to build a roadmap to an irresistible workplace? That orange blob doesn't look like any roadmap I've ever seen.

This *is* a book about culture and how to discover your company's culture. The journey isn't a perfect circle or a neat roadmap but a winding path. You won't find a one-size-fits-all map to a destination "out there" somewhere, because it's a journey of self-discovery. Finding your culture can be messy and awkward, and if you're doing it right, it's not straightforward at all. You have to start at the edges and walk toward the center to find it.

It's not an easy journey, but it's one you must take to discover the best part of what makes your people and your business unique, special, and capable of great things. I learned that the hard way by managing a really bad culture that in the end won and made really talented people incapable of working together. But in the second half of my career, I stumbled upon a great culture. As a team, we felt our way through defining our culture, and it has worked. Now that we are further along, we have a culture where people—many of whom are brand new to the workplace—can work together and share amazing accomplishments. As we have won awards and as I've been asked to speak on culture, I've looked back at the path we have taken and have laid it out in this book to help you find your way to an irresistible workplace.

Discovering your culture is necessary because culture wins. It wins every time. If you have a bad culture, it will win—and ruin your company. And if you have a great culture, it will also win and enable you to do great things.

The journey isn't an easy one; it's not symmetrical or straightforward but a journey toward the center of who your people are as a team.

I'm not a risk taker, but I'm willing to make a bet: I bet that culture will be the factor that determines your team's success in the coming years.

"Culture eats strategy for breakfast."

That famous line, attributed to Peter Drucker many years ago, is ringing true now more than ever. It's a lesson I didn't understand early in my career, and it cost me dearly. It's the backbone of how I've tried to build my team in the second half of my career. And while I don't have culture totally figured out, I am clear on this:

Culture wins.

Strategy is great. Having talented people is a must. But the real team wins come when culture is working.

When culture is bad, no matter how talented the team or great the strategy, a team will never reach its potential. Because whether good or bad, culture is the trump card that determines your team's outcome. During my early years, in a different life, I had an incredibly talented team with a good strategy and a bad culture—which was largely my fault. It didn't go well. Why? Because culture *always* wins.

CULTURE TIP

Culture always wins.

I'll never forget the first time I hired someone and felt good about it. We shook hands over a cup of coffee, and I walked away from that hire knowing I'd made the right decision for my company. More important, I'd made the right decision for my new employee. I knew he'd be happy working at my church-staffing company, Vanderbloemen Search Group.

Hiring people with the right skills has always been important to me, but it took me years to realize that, as a business owner, hiring people who would be happy working for my company was just as important—perhaps even *more* important. A good cultural fit between my company and the people who worked there didn't only improve their quality of life, but it also affected my business.

Earlier in my career, I didn't understand how important culture was to an organization's success. At thirty-one years old, I was the senior minister at the First Presbyterian Church in Houston. Sam Houston, the man who brought Texas into the United States in the nineteenth century, went to that church. Close to five thousand adults and about two thousand of their kids called First Presbyterian home. There was a school, a preschool, and hundreds of employees. It was a big church, and while I was there, the attendance grew a little and the median donor age dropped. I'm proud of the contributions I made but wish I had known then what I know now about the importance of culture in any organization. A lot of the staff left while I was the senior minister. In hindsight, I know it was because we didn't have a great culture. Worse, I know now that I was the pacesetter for that culture.

I ended up leaving the First Presbyterian Church of Houston and went to work in the corporate world for a few years before starting my own company. Hiring one person at a time, I put a lot of thought into whom I was surrounding myself with, and whom I'd be trusting with my clients. We grew organically, one hire at a time, and I slowly built a business staffed by employees who didn't just like the work but also liked working together. A culture was developing within my business, and it was the kind of culture that benefitted my employees, my clients, and me.

I Got a Surprise

One by one, I added more people to Vanderbloemen Search Group until we had grown to a legitimate business with a Houston office, a few dozen employees, and more than a hundred clients. In 2015, I was traveling for work and staying at a hotel in Baltimore when I received a phone call. It was someone from *Entrepreneur* magazine. I knew the people at my company had taken some kind of survey, and the call was about the results of the survey.

Turns out, we won best company culture in the whole country.

I was stunned. According to what the man told me, my little business didn't win the award for best culture at companies just in the city of Houston or the state of Texas, or all faith-based organizations; we were selected from all the businesses in America. I was dumbfounded. I thought for sure an award like that would go to a high-tech firm in Silicon Valley, a place with Ping-Pong tables and all-you-can-eat buffets for the employees.

After that, we won more awards and landed on more lists, including *Entrepreneur's* Top 5 Company Culture, in 2015 and 2016, and *Houston Business Journal's* Best Places to Work, in 2015 and 2016.

At first, I found it hard to believe we were being recognized nationally for something I had unintentionally stumbled upon: building an irresistible workplace. Eventually, I accepted the accolades because they represented a lot of hard work and lessons learned. Those awards represented what's possible when you realize there are many priorities to consider in building a successful company, but above all else—more than profits, more than process, and even more than people—culture wins.

Vanderbloemen Search Group's Culture Awards

Vanderbloemen Search Group won a lot of culture awards in a very short time. When people started asking me how our culture developed, I had to take a step back and look at all that we'd done to get to this place. What I discovered at my own company, and through conversations with CEOs at other companies, led me to write this book.

#1 - 2015 Entrepreneur.com's Top Company Culture list in the Small Company category[1]

#6 - 2015 Best Place to Work in Houston[2]

#3 - 2016 Best Place to Work in Houston[3]

#5 - 2016/2017 (2016 survey, results published in 2017) Entrepreneur.com's Top Company Culture list in the Small Company category[4]

I didn't set out to build an irresistible workplace that attracted top talent, so when people asked me how I did it, I didn't have a plan to share with them. I hadn't created a roadmap to an irresistible workplace, and I didn't yet understand that culture wins. To get a clear understanding of how I'd left a mediocre culture and helped create a thriving one, I thought about the choices I'd made at my company and how they were different from the choices I'd made earlier in my career. What had I done to foster a culture in which people *wanted* to work with me—and wanted to work *for* me?

First, I looked back at what happened after I left the church and went to work in the corporate world. The company was great and the money was terrific, but I wasn't happy with the work I was doing—it wasn't my calling, so to speak. While I was there, the company went through some changes. The CEO left and was replaced by another CEO within a hundred days. By church standards, a hundred-day hire was unthinkable. It took us years to replace ministry leaders. The man hired wasn't a temporary replacement either; he was a great CEO, and the company flourished under his leadership. That made me wonder what companies like that one were doing to attract and recruit talent that I and so many others weren't doing. Eventually, I quit that company and started my own business, but the question stuck in my head: How did organizations attract, recruit, and retain great people?

After leaving that company, I set up Vanderbloemen Search Group on a card table in my home. I didn't know whether my idea—a for-profit, executive search firm that helped churches find their pastor—would work, but I wanted to devote my career to a company that was aligned with my values and satisfied a niche market that had a real need. I knew firsthand, from my corporate experience, how miserable life could be working for a company that wasn't a good fit. I also knew, from my experience at First Presbyterian Church, how tough it could be for an organization to succeed if the people who worked there weren't happy. I guess I thought the pastor-recruiting-company idea would provide me with a little redemption for my past mistakes. In order to make good matchups between pastors and churches, I couldn't make the same mistakes I'd made at the church.

I started the business with no investors, no venture capital, and no debt, and I didn't plan on hiring anyone to help me. Somehow, over the years, the firm grew to forty employees. Now, people want to come to my company. They come here, they love working here, and most of them stay. The people who work for me aren't just employees; they're a "framily." That's a term I learned that refers to people who feel like friends and family in a healthy culture. In a healthy culture, the people who work with you aren't your coworkers—they're your *framily*. My employees stay longer than what I have come to see as the average tenure at a job, especially for people their age, even though some of them could find better-paying jobs. They don't join the company to hang out with their framily, though—they work hard. I have employees who come in earlier and stay later than I do because they love the company and they love the work.

What's the difference between the company we've built and a lot of other companies that aren't doing as well on the culture front? To answer that question, I researched other companies to find out what was wrong with the traditional workplace.

I also sought out CEOs of companies that had won awards for culture to see what I could learn. As it turned out, my company and theirs had similarities in our approaches and rationales for building culture, which reinforced my decisions and led to a lot of what you will read in this book.

What's Wrong at Work?

During my research, I discovered a lot of dissatisfaction in today's workplace. Two-thirds of Americans hate their jobs.[5] They don't just dislike their jobs—they literally hate them. A business where people hate their jobs can't have a healthy culture. Moreover, as a general rule, the higher the headcount—the more employees at a company—the worse the culture becomes. This makes sense because when you're starting a small business, everybody interacts face-to-face, and they all want to get along and make the company successful. There are common goals and everyone works together to reach them. However, when you have five hundred people on staff, silos develop. These siloed groups can grow apart and have conflicting goals and agendas.

Another common issue in today's workplace is that employers are having a tough time finding, attracting, and retaining employees, especially younger employees who were born from about 1980 to 2000. As of the writing of this book, these "millennials" are around twenty to forty years old. Companies have to learn how to hire and keep younger people because they don't have another choice. This is due to a phenomenon known as the "double-hump workforce," which was caused by a decrease in birth rates from around 1960 to around 1980. Baby boomers, now in their late fifties to early seventies, make up a large volume of the workforce—the first "hump"—and people born in the decades leading up to the turn of the century make up the other hump. Because fewer people were born between 1960 and 1980, there aren't enough people available who have similar work experience, longevity within a company or industry, or the qualifications to take over for retiring baby boomers. The only people who can move into those spots are those from the younger generation, so employers need to hire them, train them, and get them up to speed quickly to fill those vacant positions.

Fast-forward ten years from now, when most of the baby boomers will have left the workforce, and who is left? Companies will need to hire millennials, and they'll be in even higher demand a decade from now. Smart companies have already figured this out and are investing in their company culture as a way to build out their workforces, improve retention, and reduce attrition. Culture isn't just a feel-good idea. In this century, it may be the only way for companies to survive.

I already see this trend at my company, where 74 percent of the staff is younger than thirty-five. I don't intentionally hire people that age—they're the people who are looking for work. They didn't know one another when I hired them, but after working together, they've grown to know one another and have stayed for the friendships they've developed and for the culture we've created. We have older people here, too—people older than me. My company has economically great seasons and then it has lean seasons, but through the ups and downs, everyone stays for the culture.

Every company has a baseline culture. It's not something you map out to build but a journey of self-discovery and then self-improvement. I call that baseline culture a company's or team's *culture index*. We developed a tool for helping teams figure out their cultural index. It's a first step to identifying and creating a unique team culture that creates team wins. Again, strategy is great, but in the end, culture wins.

A company's culture index can be a good indicator of how well it's building a culture that attracts and retains employees. Although a culture index typically goes down as headcount increases, it isn't always the case. In fact, at my company, as we added people, our culture index went up. The year after winning the number-one spot for company culture in *Entrepreneur* magazine, our headcount and our culture index went up. We experienced a similar boost over time in our culture index, which was measured for the Houston's Best Places to Work award. In the fourth-largest city in the country—which has more Fortune 500 headquarters than anywhere outside of New York City—we added to our headcount and went from sixth to third place. Somehow, we bucked the trend.

That anomaly didn't escape the attention of the media, and soon after the awards were announced, I started receiving requests from publications such as *Forbes*, *Fortune*, and *Fast Company* to write about culture. Those requests forced me to take a step back and analyze how I started my business and what I did differently, especially as it related to the culture that had developed. What did I do, and what were my employees doing, that made Vanderbloemen Search Group such a great place to work?

We're All New at This

Culture isn't some new phenomenon that appeared out of nowhere, but it's changing and it's changing fast, especially in the workplace. So, in that sense, we are all new to this. How do you research something that's constantly changing? I started looking at what we were doing differently at my company, compared to other companies. I also looked at what we were doing that was similar to what other companies with successful, healthy cultures were doing, and I noticed differences and similarities. What I discovered was so fascinating that I wanted to share it.

Researching and writing helped to further clarify the process for me, and I learned even more about culture and how I'd gotten it right at my company. I hadn't started the business with a twelve-step plan in mind for building a great company culture. The culture evolved over time, and I knew the answer lay with the people—my staff. They liked working together.

As a company, my staff and I have placed a lot of people in other organizations since I started the company eight years ago, and the majority of them are still on the job. This is surprising when you consider the average tenure for a student pastor is only eighteen months. Part of our success is our vetting process. We assess the culture of an organization before we agree to recruit for it, and if it has a toxic culture, we turn down the work. I wouldn't put my family, my friends, a complete stranger, or myself in an unhealthy workplace, and I certainly don't want to profit from putting someone in that position.

I wouldn't place people at a company with an unhealthy culture, and I didn't want my own people working at one either.

Building a great culture started with the vetting and hiring process. It was as important to make sure the company was a good fit for the candidate as it was to make sure the candidate was a good fit for the company. During my research for this book, I interviewed my own staff to learn why they wanted to work for me and why they stayed. I learned that culture at my company started with hiring the right people, and it continued throughout the life cycle of their tenure with the company.

Beyond my people, I wanted to look at other companies that were winning at culture, so I interviewed about a hundred CEOs at award-winning organizations. In the process, I heard a lot of great stories about what leaders did to develop a great culture, and those are the culture wins—noun and verb, for the grammar geeks. I also learned how creating an environment with a great culture helped these companies and their people succeed. That's why I believe in culture wins (the noun) and that culture wins (verb).

Jill Donovan, the CEO of apparel design and retailer Rustic Cuff, says it best: "A positive company culture is imperative so that your employees come to the office excited to do excellent work. With their excitement comes exceptional performance, and with that performance comes happy customers." Jill started Rustic Cuff in 2011 by creating bracelets by hand for family members. The company has grown from a single employee working out of her kitchen to a business with dozens of employees; a showroom in Tulsa, Oklahoma; celebrity clients; and international sales. She credits culture as a driver for excellence, performance, and, ultimately, happy customers, and it should get the attention of every CEO who's eyeing the bottom line.

Having employees come to the office excited to work is a terrific accomplishment, but retaining them is just as important, because those people are your greatest asset. I heard this over and over again from the CEOs I interviewed. I asked them, "If you could choose between a great product, a great price point, and a great team, which would you choose for your company?" Every one of them said, "I'll take the team. It's the team that matters." They all knew, if all else failed, a great team could rebound and they could still succeed as a company. But without the team, it didn't matter how wonderful their ideas, or anything else, might be.

Having that team is critical, and keeping it matters, because losing good people affects your culture and your bottom line. When I interviewed the many CEOs at the culture-winning companies, they all told me they wanted to keep the employees they had, and to do that, they had to build a great culture. In terms of the financial piece of the equation, they knew retaining good employees was much more cost-effective than recruiting, interviewing, hiring, onboarding, training, and getting a new employee up to speed, especially given the typical learning curve of a new employee, in a new position, at a new company.

It's Not Just About Money

If you lose a good person and you don't have a replacement, you don't feel only the hard cost of hiring a search firm to help you but also the hard cost of lost productivity. When you lose a good person, the whole team feels it. They realize a talented person has moved on, and it's a blow to the team. If you've developed your culture, there's another talented person lined up to take that person's place. But if you haven't, you may be waiting a long time to fill that slot. In the meantime, there's more lost productivity, and the morale of the team takes a greater hit. The cost of losing a person and hiring a replacement is probably a lot higher than you think. In large companies, it can easily run up to six figures or more.[6]

This isn't a book about any generation of people in particular. The truth is, you have to hire people, and you'll have a higher degree of success finding good employees from any generation and keeping them working for you if you get the culture right. Culture wins, and it wins with everyone.

This book is for those young people in offices who have the ear of the CEOs. Those people are going to read this book and see the truth in it. They're going to fill it with sticky notes and highlighting to point out what they think are the most important bits. Then they're going to leave it on the CEO's desk, because they love their job and they want the company to succeed. This book is also for those people who have been working for many years and hate their job, because no one deserves that kind of life.

This book is for the human resources people who are wondering where their next recruits will come from, what they can be doing right now to attract them, and what they should be doing to hang on to the people they already have. It's for hiring managers and for anyone else who wants to see the company culture improve and believes he or she can influence the people in charge.

This book is for any leader who's wondering why it's harder to find and keep good people, and why employees stay for shorter stints and leave more frequently. That's a problem that's only going to get worse in the coming years.

This book is also written for CEOs who are looking at how they're going to attract and retain a workforce now and in the next decade. Because there's a tsunami coming.

A few years ago, I gathered all my frequent-flyer miles and took my family to Hawaii for spring break. It was the same year there was that awful earthquake in Japan. We landed on the island in the middle of the night (my flyer points were good for only the least-desirable flight time, of course), and I rented a car.

The rental-car guy said to me, "*Mahalo* [the traditional Hawaiian thank-you]. Have a nice stay, and pay attention to the tsunami warnings."

His words seemed a little odd, and I replied, "Back on the mainland, when there's a possibility of a tornado, we say there's a tornado watch. A tornado warning, on the other hand, means the tornado has been spotted and is coming—it's imminent!"

"That's right," said the rental-car guy. "It's the same thing here. The tsunami's coming. You just can't see it yet."

The guy told us to sleep in our clothes, because someone would probably wake us in the middle of the night and we'd have to evacuate. I'll never forget how I felt, hearing that—or how much fun it was (not) trying to explain it to my four-year-old son.

The earth has quaked. It quaked years ago, and the tidal waves are coming. You may not see the tsunami yet, but in the coming decade, your older employees are going to retire at a faster rate and leave an enormous vacuum of open positions you will be struggling to fill. Smart companies are investing time, money, and other resources into developing a culture right now that will provide an irresistible workplace for the new workforce. Developing that culture may not seem like an urgent matter today, but it will become a much higher priority as your people leave and there are a limited number of people to fill those positions. I see this occurring already in my recruiting efforts. Every church wants a pastor in his mid-forties to take over the place of the retiring pastor, and there aren't enough of them to go around. The tsunami is coming; you may not see it, hear it, or feel it, but it's on the horizon. Companies that aren't preparing for it right now will find it hard to survive.

Business leaders who have already figured this out—that culture wins—will want to read this book because they know about the tsunami, are preparing for it, and want to learn more. I hope people who aren't aware of the impending workforce tsunami read this book, too, because they need to get ahead of it as soon as possible.

Culture is changing and will continue to change, but you can't sit back and wait for the waves to settle. The tsunami's coming, whether you prepare for it or not, and it's time to get your feet wet. The best place to start is by looking at what companies like mine and others are doing to create an irresistible workplace where culture wins. Companies don't create culture wins by writing their values on a piece of paper and hanging it on the wall.

Values, behaviors, and everything else that comprises my company's culture evolved organically as the company grew and as more people came on board. We're still learning and improving, and I expect we always will be. But our culture comes from within, and it's driven throughout the entire organization. It's not a culture introduced to every new hire and then forgotten; it continues through the life cycle of every employee, from day one to the day he or she chooses to leave.

The day I got that call from *Entrepreneur* magazine was like a dream, but I have another dream. In it, another CEO, one who puts into practice all the lessons I'm going to teach you, gets a call. The voice on the other end tells that CEO his company just won a best-culture award. That CEO won because he took to heart the importance of building a great culture at his own company. His workplace is so irresistible, people want to work for him, and his employees don't want to leave. That CEO could be you.

GREAT TEAMS KNOW THEIR PULSE

CHAPTER 1

Why Culture Will Win in the Next Ten Years

AT MY FIRM, WE use software developed by the company HubSpot. HubSpot's specialty is content-based, inbound marketing software and services that bring customers to you so you don't have to cold-call them. Based in Boston, the company has grown quickly and won many culture awards. It has more than twenty-one thousand clients, but for some reason, it took a shine to my company and invited me to visit. I half wondered if it wanted to use Vanderbloemen Search Group as an example of what its software could do: "It's so good, it even works for this quirky little recruiting company that finds pastors for churches," or something like that.

The people at HubSpot invited me to participate in a Q&A with the CEO, Brian Halligan, at their all-staff meeting. Before I headed to Boston, I read about HubSpot's culture online. What you read about a company's culture on its website can be very different than what actually goes on at the company, so I didn't expect much.

At HubSpot, I found Brian—not in a corner office but sitting at a desk in an open workspace. I asked him where his office was, and he told me he "offices" wherever there's space. He was running a very flat organization without the typical layers of management, closed doors, or the bureaucracy that comes with that traditional corporate structure.

One of the company's values focuses on getting things done, and that is literally written on the wall in letters ten feet tall. I asked Brian how they did that—how did they "get things done"?

He told me HubSpot doesn't have a typical vacation policy: After you get your stuff done, you can go on vacation. If your stuff isn't done, you get it done. Then you go on vacation.

There were a lot of younger people working there, and I knew hiring qualified people in the very competitive tech space wasn't easy. I walked around and talked to them and asked some of them why they were there.

They said they were going to change the face of marketing—they were going to change the world. These people were more excited about saving the world with software than some pastors I knew who wanted to save the world through their church. Then I realized these people knew *why* they were there. They had a cause and a purpose they believed in, and the culture was so strong that it was palpable. They weren't just repeating the company line; they were living it.

How to Begin Thinking About Culture

Thinking about culture starts with figuring out *why* you're doing something. What's the reason behind what you do? Before you can define your cultural values, you first have to define why the company exists. What does it bring to the world? If the company went away tomorrow, would it matter? Would the world notice if it disappeared? When I spoke with the people at HubSpot, they knew exactly why they were doing what they were doing. These were coders and IT geeks, but they understood the connection between the work they did and its purpose—the end game for the company's reason for existence. "We're going to change the way sales and marketing are done, and we're going to end cold-calling."

In my fifteen years as a pastor, we talked about the "why" of our positions and our roles regularly. As a pastor, you preach about being there because the world needs hope, or Jesus, or whatever the sermon is that day. Pastors talk about the why all the time, but I wonder how common that is in today's companies. I talk about the why more now than I did as a pastor. At every staff meeting, I talk about where I saw our vision at work that week. By "vision," I mean our vision for the change we're making in the world, and that ties back to our purpose and our why. That's my job at those meetings. If you get that part right, you can build everything else around it—such as your core values, which are what you believe, and your cultural values, which are how you behave based on what you believe.

If you walked up to an admin, a salesperson, or anyone else at your company, and asked that person why he or she is there, doing what he or she is doing, what would the answer be? As CEOs, we like to tell ourselves that all of our employees understand the why behind their jobs and how their work supports that why. Step out of your office today and walk around the building. Ask people why they're there. You might be surprised by what you hear. Then sit down and figure out why *you're* there, if you haven't already, because that message has to be clearly communicated throughout the ranks before you can start working on your culture. If you're new to the power of knowing your "why," I recommend you read Simon Sinek's book, *Start with Why*.[7] Once you define your why, you have to allow it to permeate everything you do. Some companies do this very well.

Let's take Google, for example. Companies establish and follow brand guidelines for their marketing collateral, and consistency is key. They define what colors their logo can be, what font to use for the lettering, how big or small the logo can appear, and everything else about how that logo is used. Google has a core value that says, "You can have fun and wear a business suit."[8]

The story goes that the company's founders, Larry Page and Sergey Brin, went off to the Burning Man Festival, an annual gathering of artistic self-expression—and other activities—that draws tens of thousands of people from around the world. While they were away from the office, one of the employees altered the Google logo by incorporating the Burning Man, which is a simple graphic of a person with a sort of *O* as the head, into the second *O* of Google. Most companies are strict about controlling their branding, and messing with a logo is definitely not okay. But the founders had set the core value of having fun, so they allowed it. Now, Google's logo changes regularly. You can still see how it's the original logo, but it morphs with the seasons, holidays, and events, and people have fun with it. That changing logo wasn't some brilliant marketing idea—it started with a Google employee's taking a core value to heart and having fun.

Defining Culture

How do you define culture? I couldn't have answered that question in my early days as a pastor, but when I began to study it, I had an experience that illustrated culture more clearly than I could have imagined.

My perspective on culture crystalized after my oldest son started college at Texas A&M University (TAMU). He joined the school's Corps of Cadets and was quickly submerged in the TAMU culture, where people share customs and habits and pass them down from one generation to the next.

TAMU might embody the largest and most actively engaged example of culture on the planet, and nowhere is that cultural presence stronger than at Kyle Field. My first Aggies football game showed me how culture connects people across the country, from different generations, industries, and walks of life, into a powerful, cohesive unit committed to a shared goal.

When something happens at an Aggies game, the crowd roars. It's not a typical cheering crowd, though, because the fans have gathered on the field at midnight for yell practice, and they all know what to say and do and when to say and do it. Imagine ten thousand fans hollering the same yells, chants, and phrases, swaying the same way, and making the same motions and hand signals. Like a silent force, culture drives the crowd, and the feeling is palpable.

As a newcomer, I was initially overwhelmed. It was electrifying. I can't imagine how the opposing team felt. And I don't know how the Aggies ever lose a home game.

The culture at TAMU doesn't end at graduation. Those associated with the university have a family of supporters for the rest of their lives, because they're part of a strong network of people who've accepted the Aggie culture, and it's a lifelong bond.

So, what exactly is culture? Here is a frequently cited definition (it's one of my favorites). Ironically, I came across it in a paper by a professor at TAMU, which is arguably the largest cult(ure) on the planet:

> *A culture is a way of life of a group of people—the behaviors, beliefs, values, and symbols that they accept, generally without thinking about them, and that are passed along by communication and imitation from one generation to the next.*[9]

What if companies had behaviors, beliefs, values, and symbols they accepted and passed on from one generation of workers to the next? Wouldn't that create an empowered workforce and an irresistible workplace? What if companies understood culture and could define it, create it, and nurture it within their own organizations? How powerful would that be?

My First Thoughts on Culture

My first thoughts on building a company culture weren't front and center for me until after I had worked in a church and at a for-profit company, and then decided to start my own business. When I started my firm, I didn't set out to build a great culture. In fact, I didn't know what a great culture even looked like, but I knew from experience what it *didn't* look like.

The church I had come from was a wonderful place, but it had a terrible culture and part of that was my fault. The oil and gas company was wonderful, too—an impressive organization where the pay was good and the people were good, but the culture just didn't click with me. While I was there, I learned what "Hump Day" meant and why everyone looked forward to getting past the middle of the week—and closer to the weekend. I started counting the days until my next vacation.

I wanted to leave that company, and at the same time, I wanted to do something to help churches. One day, I came home from work and told my wife I wanted to quit my job. This was 2008, by the way, which was a very bad time to be quitting any job. I didn't realize we were at the beginning of the Great Recession. I had just gotten married and bought a house, and my wife and I had six kids between us from previous marriages. I was going to quit my job at the oil and gas company and start my own business because I had a new idea for churches, and as everyone knows, *churches just love new ideas* (said no one ever in the history of churches).

I wasn't thinking about culture at the time; I was thinking about how I was going to convince churches that it was wise to spend money on hiring people, which is something they had never done. I quit my job, convinced enough churches to hire me, and a company was born. As I added more people, our culture was born, too.

I started with just one employee, me, and we agreed on everything. It's amazing how wonderful the culture can be when there are no other people to consider. But as I started hiring people, it became clear to me that if I wanted to avoid creating a culture I didn't want—the kind I'd experienced in my previous jobs—I needed to pay close attention to the people I was hiring.

I hired Holly Tate to help out with business development. She was smart, positive, and energetic, and she fit the culture I *did* want. Holly was the kind of person I wanted working at my firm. More important, she *wanted* to work for me.

I asked Holly a lot of questions about why she wanted the job. It wasn't the specific work, the location, the money, or anything else I expected to hear—she was personally committed to our goal of finding pastors for churches, and she liked how we were doing it. That's when I got my first glimmer of an idea as to the kind of culture I wanted: a culture where people weren't showing up because it was their job, or just for the pay, but because they wanted to be here. They wanted to be doing what we were doing, the way we were doing it.

What if, I thought, *I hired only people who wanted—really wanted—to do this kind of work, at this kind of company, the way we were doing it, and with these kinds of people? What kind of culture would that inspire?*

I started thinking about this with every new hire. Within six months, I had doubled my staff. A culture was developing.

What I Learned About Culture

When I got that call telling me my company had won the best-culture award, I wondered how we had won out of all the other great companies out there. Bay Area tech companies were attracting tens of thousands of employees, and they had racquet-ball courts, yoga classes, and all the food you could eat. Here we were, this little start-up. We were thirty people crammed into five thousand square feet in an office barely a step above slum status. When I hired people, they got an IKEA desk and they had to build it. Don't laugh—it's true! Somehow, that didn't matter to my people, because they were happy to be there. We were all happy to be there because we had an irresistible culture.

You don't have to be a giant company to have a great culture. You don't have to be in the tech industry, or located in Silicon Valley, or have tens of thousands of employees or a Ping-Pong table. You have to commit to building and being part of a framily that embraces what you're trying to accomplish and how you're going to get there.

Moreover, culture isn't a lesson taught from the top down. It can come from anyone in your organization. It's not the person with the biggest title telling the guy in the cubicle what to do or how to think, or the older woman with the most seniority telling the new woman how to do her job. In an irresistible workplace, cultural standards, ideas, and mentoring flow freely among everyone, without regard for who's "in charge." Cultural mores aren't the domain of the senior minority; they're open to discussion, debate, and expansion by all.

Eventually, I created my own definition of culture, which is this:

Culture is about how a team uniquely functions when it's at its best. It's about how you function as a team when you're working well. It's about knowing the habits, customs, and mannerisms that are common to your team but uncommon to other teams. And ultimately, building an effective culture means knowing, memorializing, and embedding them as cultural values the team is expected to live by.

How you get there starts with communication, but not the typical communication in which the CEO commands employees. Cultural communication is about asking questions.

At the end of each day, I don't ask myself, "How many times did I tell people what to do today?" Instead, I ask, "How many times did I ask people how *they* want to do their jobs today?" This doesn't insinuate a weak style of leadership. Rather, by engaging people and allowing them a voice, leadership is enhanced. As CEO, you aren't Moses coming off the mountain with the Ten Cultural Commandments. Those commandments are at the base of the mountain with the people, and if you ask your people questions, you'll discover what they are. Culture is a crowdsourced activity, and your employees are the crowd.

When you're defining culture, don't look only to your senior advisers for help. They should certainly be involved in the conversation, but if you're building a company culture for the next decade and beyond, you need to listen to what the young people in your company have to say. They're the people who'll be running your business in the coming years, and they need to have a voice in how the culture develops and evolves.

Culture and Retention

Right now, culture is the key to retaining employees, especially younger employees. Their lives are different than mine was at that age. They're getting married later and starting families later.[10] They're more likely to move away from their parents and siblings, so there's no one waiting for them at home.[11] Their families are the people in the office, their framilies.

I was struck by this one Thanksgiving when I saw an Instagram post of my employees eating dinner together. My wife, Adrienne, asked, "What are they all doing eating together? Don't they have families?" Yes, I told her, they are a family.

Another difference that sets the new generation of employees apart from their predecessors is their desire to work for a cause over money. I've had people take a cut in pay to work for me because they believed in our mission. Having a cause they believe in—not a goal based on profits, but a service that helps others succeed or helps the world become a better place—is very important to these people. Elon Musk has been known to say that he's not building just another car; he's interested in building one that's going to use less fossil fuel, change the climate, and change the way this world does transportation. Do you think younger people want to work at his company, Tesla, or at a car company with an outdated mission that neglects this worldview?

Market researcher Barna Group did a survey asking people what they wanted to accomplish by the time they were thirty-five years old. They asked people in the 1920s, '30s, '40s, '50s, '60s, '70s, and into the 1980s, and in every decade, the responses were consistent. People said they wanted to get married, start a family, own a home, be on a career path that would last, and have financial security. If you ask millennials that question, the only answer they provide of those five is, "I want to have financial security." They're not thinking about a career path or having a family and a home. They have a different mindset, and that mindset is taking over the workplace. They attach more significance to what they do with their time—a large part of that being their work—than any other generation before them. Therefore, knowing what you and your company stand for, and creating a culture that reflects what you stand for, is essential to attracting that workforce.

Culture unifies and self-guides a team toward an overall mission. Management doesn't "police" the mission—the staff police themselves and hold themselves accountable to the cultural standards they have created and accepted. When you see that happening at your company, your people will do their best work and your organization will be at its highest level of performance and productivity. When you aren't the only one talking about the mission or the vision, and your people start preaching the message among themselves, you know culture is winning. People will own it, adhere to it, nurture it, and share stories about how they witnessed the company's values and culture in action.

I've heard it said many times, and the longer I work with talent, the more I believe it: "People don't leave jobs; they leave managers." It's true, but if you have a bad culture, people won't stay either. People leave bad leaders and managers—those who traditionally set culture—and they leave bad cultures. If the culture's good, they're more likely to stay.

What Other Companies Doing Culture Right Think

During my research for this book, I interviewed people who had made a concerted effort to build a good culture. These weren't typical corporate leaders but people who took culture seriously and had changed the way their companies work by focusing on culture. I asked them why they were doing it—why were they pouring so much money into their company's culture? I got the same answer over and over again: retention. They knew keeping a good employee is easier and less expensive than trying to replace one.

Unfortunately, most companies underestimate the financial value of culture. They think throwing resources at it is a waste of time and money. The fact is, losing good people is expensive, and as I mentioned earlier, trying to replace them is expensive.

A culture that promotes retention has a solid return on investment. Melissa Allen, who is the CEO and co-owner of internet marketing company GetUWired, told me, "With improved employee surveys, we reduced turnover and training costs." Those costs went down because the culture improved and good people stayed, helping to train the new people who came on board.

Retention at Vanderbloemen Search Group

No matter how good your company culture is, some people will leave, but they'll leave for different reasons. At my company, Vanderbloemen Search Group, not everyone stays. I have had people leave for personal reasons such as starting a family or moving across the country. They weren't running away from the business or the culture but toward something else that had become a higher priority in their life.

Most of the people who left my firm helped find their replacement and train them, too. With the former employees' permission, we keep their names on a list of references, so when we're interviewing a new person who wants to know what it's like to work at the firm, we can provide that list. If you've got a great culture, a fair percentage of your former employees should be willing to act as references for your company, for future hires.

Past employees of my company, like an "extended framily," still stop by now and then for a cup of coffee and to say hello to everyone.

What I have learned from seeing some people leave is, you can't take their decision personally and you should support them. If my company's culture provided them with a place to work that they enjoyed for a while, then I consider our time together a success. My best hope is that they move on to a place that fits their current needs in life, and they'll take some of what they learned about culture at my company with them to their next workplace.

Culture and Start-Ups

Culture is often associated with start-up companies, and there's a sort of start-up fever going on right now.

In 2016, Stanford University's business school had more graduates planning to go into start-ups than investment banking.[12] Even before graduation, business majors are looking to start-ups for cultural inspiration. MBA students line up to intern at companies such as financial-tech start-up Earnest, citing culture as a major motivator: "For the interns, what makes Earnest special isn't just 'next generation' banking techniques—it's being a critical part of a culture that embraces change and impact…truly making the world a better place and delivering value, and internally, for people being truly fulfilled with their work and doing their best work every day and making value."[13]

Start-up fever has even affected the church world. Not long ago, a person would finish Bible college or seminary school and become a student pastor looking forward to eventually rising to the position of senior pastor at an established church. Now almost everybody comes out of school wanting to start his or her own church.

Start-ups might be the best places to study culture because they can build it from day one and allow it to evolve as they add employees. It's difficult to go into an established company and try to change the culture overnight. Starting my own company allowed me to get the culture right, while I don't know whether I would have ever figured it out when I was senior pastor at First Presbyterian.

If you want to learn firsthand how a company creates a great culture, talk to someone who's done it at a start-up. For example, Kieran Mathew of Amplify Solutions wanted to start a company that did marketing for products targeted at college-aged students. In order to ensure his company's offerings would attract this demographic, Kieran built his company around a handful of full-time employees, and then hired about seventy contract employees, who were all college students. He has a collaborative culture with students from many different campuses working together to fulfill the company's vision. How does he get all those different people around the country to work together? He does it with a culture that promotes collaboration and flexibility and supports the remote contract worker. When you get the culture right, you have more choices about whom you hire and how your company operates, because your workforce is on board and willing to work together to make it happen.

Why Culture Trumps Competency

Culture trumps competency, and nowhere is that more apparent than in our intern program. I didn't intend to hire interns, but when a lot of tasks started piling up that no one seemed to have time for, or was excited to do, I asked my son to step in and give us a hand. He, in turn, referred a friend to us, to give us more help. They were both too young and inexperienced to land a high-paying job, but as interns, they got a feel for what it was like to work at the firm, and we got an idea of what it was like to have them on board.

They didn't come in with the competencies we needed, but they fit the culture, and they learned all the required skills during their internships. Now, we bring on several interns every year, and that program has become a pipeline for new hires. We rotate the interns through the departments so they have a chance to discover their talents and interests, and if they're a good fit, once they graduate from college, we often end up hiring them. Our intern-to-hire ratio is high, nearly 100 percent. We've found that if people are a good cultural fit, we can teach them the competencies. On the other hand, people who come in with all the skills they need to do a job won't necessarily be a good fit with the culture of the company.

Intern programs are a low-risk hiring strategy for businesses, because the financial investment is low and there's no expectation on the part of the intern for permanent employment. They're a great method for testing out a person's cultural fit and ability to learn new skills, too. While you need experienced, skilled people at your company, consider bringing on an intern occasionally. You may be surprised by how quickly people who fit your company's culture can get up to speed on everything they need to know to do their job.

Internships solved a problem at my company, and they also supported our values of "solution-side living" and "ever-increasing agility," while protecting our company culture. Leveraging your values to solve problems can reinforce those values, because you have an opportunity to prove to yourself, again, why they're so valuable, and why they make your company a better place to work.

Another hiring method I've used is the ninety-day contract. If an experienced candidate does well during the interview process, and you believe he or she is a great cultural fit—but doesn't have all the competencies—offer the job on a contractual basis. Ninety days is enough time to figure out if someone really is a good fit, and it allows the person to learn the skills required to do the job. At the end of the contract, you can decide whether or not to offer a permanent position.

Why Culture Will Win

Culture will win. It already is winning. It's the glue that holds your company together as everything else changes, and those changes are going to keep coming faster and faster.

I tend to agree with change expert Ray Kurzweil, who says change is about to snowball. He writes, "We're entering an age of acceleration. The models underlying society at every level, which are largely based on a linear model of change, are going to have to be redefined. Because of the explosive power of exponential growth, the 21st century will be equivalent to 20,000 years of progress at today's rate of progress; organizations have to be able to redefine themselves at a faster and faster pace."[14]

Technology is changing the way we live and work. Job-hopping, career-hopping, and moving geographically for work aren't about to slow down. If you don't like the rate of change now, hang on and don't give up. Amid all the change, you can take action to attract and retain people, and help your company survive. While the people—your employees—may come and go, you can build a culture that bends with the changes.

Your people, no matter how happy they are, are going to leave eventually. Every employee is an interim employee, but your culture will remain. If it's a good culture, you'll keep attracting and retaining new people who will be happy to work for you.

Culture remains, and a good culture continues as a bond for the people who move on. That's why my son, who recently graduated from TAMU, can sit down and have a conversation with a much older friend of my mother-in-law's who also went to TAMU. They talk as if they've known each other their whole lives because they share a common culture. That's how culture sustains and transcends the longevity of the time a student puts in at the school—or an employee puts in at the workplace. That's also why, no matter who comes through your company, when you get the culture figured out, founded, established, and driven through the organization, the culture will carry on, like it does at TAMU.

If you're wondering what culture looks like, keep in mind that culture looks different at every company, because every company is different. Industries are different. What works in one place, for one group of people, may not work in another. Innovation, risk, fun, and creativity might work great for a video game company but may not be successful at an accounting firm. You probably don't want to hear your neurosurgeon say, "Hey, guys, let's try something new!" Culture will look different at each workplace and there's only one cardinal rule: You have to be agile. Agility—being able to pivot, move, and shift with the rapid changes—will allow your culture to bend, swerve, and survive. If you aren't agile, you'll be left behind.

That's the why behind culture—why your company's success in the coming decade begins with a great culture. You can't just tack it on to what you're doing right now. Culture starts with a healthy foundation upon which you build.

CHAPTER 2

Foundation for a Healthy Workplace

I MOVED TO HOUSTON IN Fall 2001 to pastor First Presbyterian Church.

When people outside the city asked me about Houston, I told them it was a city of innovation.

"If you want innovation in the space industry, come to Houston—we've got the Space Center. If you want innovation in making cancer history, come to Houston—we've got MD Anderson Cancer Center. If you want innovation in sports arenas, come to Houston—we've got the Astrodome. If you want innovation in accounting," I told people, "we have Enron."

Many community leaders attended First Presbyterian, including Enron CEO Jeff Skilling and whistleblower Sherron Watkins. At the time, their company was starting to come apart at the seams.

When you walked through the Enron building, you saw their four core values, "integrity, communication, respect, and excellence," written boldly in the lobby so everyone could see them upon entering and exiting work every day. The words implied the company was built upon those values. Yet, Enron—at the time, the seventh-largest company in the world—fell apart because it had a shaky foundation built on distrust.[15]

As a young pastor, I was amazed by Enron's story. This company was filled with educated, professional people, but its unhealthy culture led management and employees to see unethical behavior and look the other way. It was one of the biggest corporate disasters in US history. Enron was in the right city—the city of innovation. It had the most talented people working in the coolest building, yet its lack of a culture based on ethical values led to its downfall in a very short time.[16]

It was hard for me to imagine an organization that didn't consider ethics and morality high among its core values, but after speaking with many CEOs about workplace culture, it occurred to me that my company had an unfair advantage. By virtue of our mission—which is to serve churches—my firm attracts people who have a foundation based on ethical core values. This same foundation is not necessarily found in other companies, because every industry and organization has a different mission and attracts different kinds of people. This realization led me to wonder whether developing a great culture was the result of my intentional focus on that outcome, or if I had simply "lucked out" because values-driven people wanted to work for me. I believe our culture developed as a result of a combination of the two.

However it came to be, I learned you can't build a healthy culture on a shaky foundation, and you can't be complacent and expect your company's culture to remain healthy without regular maintenance and occasional intervention. A solid foundation relies on basic cultural health, but the deeper requirement is a code of human decency among everyone in the organization.

Basic Cultural Health

Bryan Miles, cofounder of BELAY, started his virtual-executive-assistant company at the same time I started my staffing firm. BELAY has a no-gossip policy. Because his employees are all virtual, this might seem like an unusual policy, but even virtual employees are in constant contact with one another via phone, email, conference calls, and virtual collaboration sites such as Slack, Skype, and Teamwork. At Bryan's company, if you gossip, you're done. His intent with this policy is to anchor the culture in a common morality.

Bryan also doesn't allow anonymous company surveys, because he feels if people aren't willing to own their criticism by putting their name on it, he doesn't want to hear the complaints. Does this mean you should never do anonymous surveys related to company culture? No. In fact, we do them at my firm. But to Bryan and his company, transparency with one another—rather than anonymous surveys and gossip—is very important.

A healthy culture is reflected in how people view the company, the work, and one another—and in how they treat one another. You might think identifying a healthy or a toxic culture is easy and obvious, but unless you're privy to every conversation and interaction—and if you are the CEO, I can guarantee you are not—you may have no idea what state your company's culture is in. To get an idea of where your organization stands on the culture front, ask yourself these questions.

Question 1: Is there a basic code of human decency?

The Golden Rule is a simple, straightforward tenet by which you can gauge your company's basic code of human decency: "Do unto others as you would have them do unto you." In other words, treat others like you want to be treated. When you look at your company's culture, does it follow this rule, or does it reflect a cutthroat mentality? Companies that punish low performance and offer high rewards for sales or other measurements of productivity often lean toward a cutthroat culture, because the system encourages employees to focus on their own best interests. If you're in a high-risk, high-reward industry, ask yourself whether your people are being decent to one another, or if the reward system is promoting self-serving behavior and an unhealthy culture.

The Golden Rule is so all-encompassing and easy to apply that it can practically be used as a litmus test in most situations for gauging the health of your company's culture.

Question 2: Do people like working here?

Your employees won't always tell you whether they're happy or unhappy, but if you talk to your people regularly, asking them questions about their work and paying attention to their responses and body language, you should have a general idea of their attitude toward you, their coworkers, the work, and the company.

Going back to the Golden Rule, if you were one of your employees, would you like working for yourself at your company? One sure-fire test for determining how people feel about their job is whether or not they're referring their friends to you. If your best employees are bringing in referrals, it's a safe bet they like working at your company. After all, who would refer a friend or family member to a company they didn't like?

This brings us to the next question, which may be the biggest litmus test of your company culture.

Question 3: Are the best people (not slackers) referring their friends to work at the company?

Hiring through referrals is a growing trend.[17] Anyone can look good on paper, but a résumé or curriculum vitae provides no information about work ethic or other factors that influence an employee's performance and cultural style. Referrals from your top employees are attractive candidates. Within my search group and through interactions with consultants, I've seen a waning interest in the value of résumés and a growing affinity for the networking community that can refer you. Some of my best employees have come from internal referrals.

Are your best people referring their friends to you? That's the ultimate test of cultural satisfaction. Just as you would recommend a great restaurant to a friend, wouldn't you also recommend a great employer to people you like? Likewise, you would probably warn your friends away from a bad restaurant or a company with an unhealthy culture.

If your top people aren't bringing in new candidates, ask yourself, why not?

If you were an employee of your company, would you refer *your* friends to work there?

Question 4: Do people trust the leadership of the organization?

At the close of the 1800s, Heinz, the ketchup company, was close to bankruptcy when it unveiled a new product at the World's Fair. The new ketchup was packaged in octagonal glass bottles. At that time, this was a courageous move, because factory laws weren't as rigorous as they are today, and companies didn't want people to see the processed food inside the jars they were purchasing. Heinz's transparent packaging allowed consumers to see exactly what they were getting. That move may have saved the company.[18]

Transparency builds trust. Just as Heinz was transparent about its product with its customers, to build trust, leaders have to be transparent with their employees. When you want people to trust you, you have to be willing to share more than you're used to, and being transparent may require sharing financials or other information with your employees that you may not be comfortable sharing.

At the same time, you can measure how much your team trusts its leaders by how comfortable they are with *not* knowing every little detail.

The leadership at my company shares a lot with employees in an effort to be transparent, but our staff doesn't push to know all the details. It's a two-way street. When leadership is transparent and the culture is healthy, the team has a level of trust in its leaders, believing they'll do what's right when it matters most. The talk around my company's water cooler isn't about what the leadership is up to, and our employees aren't constantly questioning, worrying, or gossiping among themselves about the state of the business. We share openly and strive for transparency, so they don't have to. We treat them the way we like to be treated.

If you have a new company, there's a lot of opportunity for setting the culture right now, while you're choosing your leaders. You can change the culture over time, but it's harder to make changes as your company grows and more people come on board. The culture at Ford Motor Company was set a long time ago, while the culture for Tesla is being set more recently by one guy, Elon Musk, and his four direct reports.

If people don't trust the leadership at your company, consider how the top five people in the organization measure up with these questions. Do they follow a basic code of human decency and treat others the same way they want to be treated? Do they like their job? After you review the remaining questions in this section, think about how your top five stack up and whether they reflect these thirteen areas of a healthy culture. If you're not seeing it at the top, then there's a problem. The easiest way to figure out a company's culture is by looking at the top five people in the organization.

If the people at the top don't embody a healthy culture, your people won't trust them, and your mission and vision statements will be irrelevant. Words don't set a culture, but people do.

Question 5: Are people communicating with one another at work?

Healthy communication looks different depending on the industry, company, and department. For example, our sales and marketing teams have very different dynamics compared to our research team. When we first moved into a new office, the sales team was one big happy family. Space was tight, but the team didn't mind, because they needed to communicate often. Likewise, the marketing team interacted frequently and openly.

The research team, on the other hand, was very quiet. They wore headphones and worked individually, for the most part. Their communication was usually one-on-one and not at all like the sales and marketing teams' open discussions.

Putting the research team next to the marketing team was a disaster. The marketing team members were always discussing new ideas and sharing their thoughts out loud—and usually quite loudly. It wasn't that everyone was talking all the time—that's not a healthy form of communication. They were, however, communicating with one another openly, regularly, and effectively, which is necessary in sales and marketing. That form of communication didn't work for the researchers, who prefer texting and group chat. The marketing department's communication was interfering with the research department's work, and so we moved the teams apart. Now, when people from marketing have to speak with people in research, they know they have to be a littler quieter than they're used to in that team's space.

Part of our culture is striving to understand one another's personalities and communication preferences, so we know how to best serve each other. A team's or an individual's communication preferences can vary broadly, not just in medium—such as verbal versus email, text, or chat—but in duration as well. Some companies use a personality inventory to determine each person's preferred style and method of communicating with others. At my company, we identify communication preferences with a program called Insights Discovery, which determines, in order of preference, the four primary drivers for each person's personality. Using oversized, foam Lego-style blocks to represent each communication style, we stack them in order of individual preference on each person's desk, so everyone knows the best way to approach their coworkers.

For example, I have an action-oriented personality, so my blocks are stacked red, yellow, blue, and green. That doesn't mean anything to a person who hasn't taken the Insights Discovery training, but my people understand that the best way to communicate with me is to research their ideas before they bring them to me, give me a brief overview, and if there's something I need to read as a follow-up, leave it with me to review at a later time. I don't mind if they blow into my office with a bright idea and depart just as quickly—in fact, I prefer it. That's how I communicate, and work, best.

Of course, I do have meetings, conferences, and other interactions that last much longer, but if people need to come by my desk to ask me a question or share an idea, they know I'll be more receptive if they're prepared with a succinct question or comment.

Generally speaking, if I need to speak with our head of marketing, I allow a full seven minutes or longer for the conversation to be effective. At the far end of the spectrum, members of our research staff might require a twenty-minute window. A research conversation is less likely to happen on a walk-in basis and is more effective if we schedule time together so we can go over everything that requires our attention.

Finally, a conversation with an engineer might take minutes—or days. The conversation is done when it's done, so if I don't have any flexibility in my schedule, it's best for me to not talk to an engineer until I have that flexibility. I'm stereotyping here, obviously, but different roles in a company attract different people with different personality types, and once you recognize the communication style of the people with whom you interact, you can adapt to their style, and they to yours.

Now we use Insights Discovery as part of our onboarding process, which is covered in more detail in chapter 7.

Whatever method your team uses to communicate is irrelevant, as long as it works and is effective. If team members are not communicating, you have a culture problem. If they're not *fully* communicating—caring enough to discover one another's preferences and be willing to adapt to them—then you have a culture problem. As a leader, you have a responsibility to uncover your employees' communication styles and preferences, and figure out if they're having meaningful, effective conversations that enable them to be productive and enjoy their work. If that isn't happening, you may have bigger problems down the road.

Question 6: How much are you collaborating?

Healthy communication opens the door to collaboration, where your people are working together as a team. How much are your people collaborating? Communication affects collaboration, and so do other factors, such as schedules and workspace. If your workspace is a cubicle farm where everyone is isolated from one another, you're probably not seeing a lot of collaboration. You can promote more collaboration with an open-plan workspace, with no walls, or one with low walls so people can see and speak to one another freely.

Of course, the degree of collaboration required differs, depending on the work. Engineers, accountants, and other people who need to focus on their individual work for long periods without interruption will probably prefer some isolation, and when they need to collaborate, they can get together in a conference room. For example, my company's controller prefers to sit in the farthest corner of the office, away from everyone else. I have an accountant who would die if I made her sit in the middle of the room. People who handle sensitive information, such as personnel files, aren't going to be very pleased—or productive—with an audience, so their collaboration will be much different than, say, the collaboration of a sales team.

A healthy culture isn't symbolized by employees with their heads down, quietly pounding away at the work all day, but it doesn't rely on constant chatter and socializing either. Rather, regular, effective communication and collaboration symbolize and promote the kind of culture you need in your company, so be aware when those activities aren't happening.

Question 7: Are you innovating, or working the way you always have?

At the beginning of this chapter, we talked about Enron. The company was innovating but not with the best intentions and certainly not per the Golden Rule. Innovations in accounting methods still have to follow certain rules, and while Enron's example isn't one I recommend, any company, in any industry, should be asking itself, "How can we improve this? How can we do this better, make this better, or serve our customers better? How do we innovate?"

Falling into the "this is the way we've always done it" trap leads to complacency, boredom, and a lack of excitement and will sink your culture. Of all the CEOs I interviewed for this book—and remember, these are leaders of award-winning, culture-winning organizations—not one told me, "We don't change very much here. Innovation isn't what we do."

Change has always been a constant in life, and today, change is happening faster than ever before. For example, as I was writing this book, the iPhone turned ten years old. That technology has had such a dramatic effect on our businesses and our lives—from texting to handheld web access and email, selfies to apps—yet ten years ago, it didn't even exist. Considering all the rapid change happening all around us, companies unwilling to innovate will quickly calcify and lose the culture game. If you're not innovating, you're dying.

Question 8: Are employees supported with the tools they need to do what they need to get done?

Again, remember the saying "People don't leave companies; they leave managers." Why do people quit managers? People are unhappy and often quit because they're asked to do a job but aren't provided with the tools to get it done.

For example, my salespeople like to talk with their hands. I don't know if this is true of all salespeople, but mine stand up when they're on the phone, and they wave their hands in the air while they talk. Inevitably, they get tangled up in their own phone cords and yank their headphones off. It's funny to watch, but not a very effective way for them to hold a phone conversation.

I wanted to make it easier for the salespeople to do their jobs, so I ordered AirPods for all of them. The little wireless earphones allow them to walk, talk, and gesticulate to their hearts' content, without missing a beat. Other people on our team need quiet stages to conduct interviews, and the open-office concept we have doesn't work for their needs. To accommodate these people, we have private phone booths around the perimeter of the room.

When I'm asking people to spend their time on the phone all day to accomplish a job, I intentionally make the effort to make the work comfortable for them. If they can't keep their headphones on or can't find a quiet place to conduct a phone interview, it's up to me to remedy those issues for them. We'll talk more about the physical space you provide for employees and how it affects culture in chapter 4, "Great Culture, Top to Bottom."

Ask yourself whether your employees feel supported. If they're asked to build a website, are you giving them the computer and the software to allow them to build it? If they're asked to take on a creative project, do you micromanage them or keep them from having the flexibility to be creative?

Look at what you ask of your employees, then ask yourself if you're providing them with everything they need to do their jobs, and do them well. This includes tools such as hardware and software, time, a good workspace, a supportive working environment, and potentially even training and more people to support their success.

Question 9: Do people take responsibility and ownership for their work?

A pastor friend of mine says that in life, people fall on one of two sides of the equation: the problem side or the solution side.

In an unhealthy work culture, people blame others, talk about what happened to them, how they were wronged, and how they *would* have gotten something done…*but*. These people sound like Eeyore when he lost his tail.

In other cultures, you'll hear people say, "How can we solve the problem? How do we make it better?" It's like working in a room full of Tiggers. This doesn't mean a group of pessimists create a bad culture. It's exactly the opposite: A bad culture will breed a bunch of pessimists. It will also encourage people to shift blame, instead of taking responsibility and ownership for their actions and their work.

I've worked with people who, when they made a mistake, simply admitted it and apologized. Rather than making excuses for themselves and their actions, which would have left everyone around them feeling angry, disappointed, or uncomfortable, they accepted responsibility for errors, allowing everyone to move on with the work.

Question 10: Space matters. Do people like the space they're in?

Do your people like the space they work in, or do they feel like they're trapped in a cell with a bare lightbulb dangling over their heads? An inviting workspace where people are comfortable and energized can lift your culture more than you might think.

There's a lot you can do to create an environment where people are excited to come to work, and it doesn't have to involve installing sliding boards between floors, like on the show *Silicon Valley*, or putting in a giant Ping-Pong table, like you might see at a company such as Google. You need to provide a comfortable, clean, nicely lit workspace that allows your team to live out the company's cultural values.

Our group is one of the smallest companies in our building, located on one of the smallest floors, and we have IKEA furniture. Having a great culture isn't defined by cool, trendy fixtures; it's about having a workspace you enjoy coming to every day. If the people on your team don't like where they're sitting, great work and motivation are hard to come by.

As a guy who started his own business on a shoestring, I am violently opposed to overhead. I hate it. However, the money I put into my company's workspace pays for itself, because my people enjoy the place, and they enjoy coming to work.

We started in an even smaller place, but as our team grew, we had to find more room. We looked at a lot of old-school office buildings that were basically cubicle farms—row after row of putty-colored, fabric cells. Wooden doors lined the perimeter,

hiding individual offices where the management was supposed to rule—or hide, I suppose. The design of these cubicle farms made it impossible for people to communicate, collaborate, or do any kind of work at all together, which doesn't work well for a search firm.

We finally found a space with glass walls. My office is glass, so while I'm working, I can see everyone working and they can see me. There might be four people from three different teams sitting together, on their laptops, and occasionally looking up to communicate with one another as they work. They move around as needed and intentionally seek one another out to help solve their problems. Their open workspace lends itself to collaboration within and among teams, so they can be more productive and enjoy the work.

Look around your office. Is there space for people to communicate and collaborate, or is everyone tucked away in a cube? Would you enjoy working in their workspace?

Question 11: Is there alignment between the service you provide and the organization's values?

At my company, our tagline is, "We staff the church." We help values-driven organizations grow further and faster by matching the right team members to their needs. Most of our values align with the values of the organizations we provide services to.

If your organization's values do not align with what you're actively doing, you're going to experience tremendous problems. Think about the situation with Travis Kalanick, founder and former CEO of Uber. He was caught yelling at one of his own employees on camera.[19] His service, driving people where they want to go, can be successful only if his drivers are friendly and ethical, yet, based on his behavior, who can believe the company's culture supports those high ideals?

When the values of your company don't align with the service you're providing, great culture is extremely difficult.

Question 12: Does your organization have *sustained* high turnover?

You've probably been told if you have a high employee turnover rate, then you must have a bad company culture. However, study after study shows, while constant turnover *can* be an issue, a spike in turnover over a short period of time doesn't necessarily mean you have an unhealthy culture.[20]

Let me explain. I used to keep a book on my desk titled *What Got You Here Won't Get You There*,[21] and I kept it there to remind myself, as I had a growing organization in a changing field, that my staff will change. People grow and change, and their personal and professional goals change. It's not uncommon for an employee who's doing killer work to decide to leave a company for another job or for personal reasons. People will leave to pursue other opportunities, and they'll leave when your company is no longer a good fit for them.

Not long ago, one of my best people came to me and said, "The company keeps growing faster, and I can't go any faster than I already am. I'm at a new season in life, and I'll probably need to step off the bus." This doesn't mean our company has a bad culture, or the person who left is bad.

Deciding to part ways isn't shameful, for an individual or for a company. As a company grows, the demands on the employees change, and your people might not be able to—or might not want to—always change with it. Also, as people grow and change, because they get married, start families, or their spouse gets a new job and they decide to move across the country, their goals no longer fit with what the company needs from them. Nevertheless, focusing on the turnover rate you're experiencing would be a mistake, especially considering the massive influx of millennials—who tend to change jobs more frequently than their predecessors[22]—into the workforce.

While a spike in turnover doesn't necessarily mean you have a culture problem, if no one on your staff has been there for more than a couple of years, you need to start asking questions. Over the next twenty years, employees will remain in the same job for shorter times, due to the change in the workforce and in the work environment. Fast-growing start-ups might have an even higher turnover, and any company growing quickly can expect to lose people in short spurts, but a high attrition rate isn't a red flag unless it's sustained.

The bottom line is, although conventional wisdom says turnover equals culture problem, it's not always true. Consider your company's situation and the situations of your employees, and decide if you have a culture problem or are simply experiencing growing pains in your company or in your workforce. Pay attention to the overall turnover, but don't be enslaved by it.

Question 13: Does your company actively encourage and reward you for taking care of your nonwork life?

All the companies I researched provide their employees with resources to help them improve and maintain their physical fitness. My employees receive a free gym membership. In addition, a trainer comes into the office once a week, and the time my people spend working out is paid time, so they don't have to squeeze it into their lunch hour. Each year we have some type of fitness challenge. Like most companies with a healthy culture, we're interested in whether our employees take care of themselves.

Of course, the nonwork-life category goes beyond gym memberships and exercise. For example, many companies have changed their vacation and sick-time policies, so if you want to go to your daughter's dance recital or have lunch with your spouse, you can take an extended lunch. You don't have to take a whole day of vacation time to do something either; instead, you can take blocks of hours off and then still work part of the day. There's a focus on quality of life at work and outside the office.

For our team, we're not big believers in the virtual workspace. However, because we live in a big city with arguably the worst commute in the country, people can choose their work hours. They might want to work from 7:00 a.m. to 4:00 p.m. so they can spend more time with their children after school, or they may choose to work from 10:00 a.m. to 7:00 p.m. so they can avoid rush-hour traffic. My employees can change their hours as their needs change. We have a core set of hours, from

10:00 a.m. to 3:00 p.m., where everyone is in the office, but if someone wants to come in at 5:00 a.m. to work out in our gym, then be at their desk at 6:00 a.m. so they can leave the office before the traffic gets bad, they can. Offering flexibility to people improves their quality of life outside the office so they can be happier when they're at work.

Warning Signs of a Poor Culture

If you answered yes to the above questions, you probably have a pretty healthy culture. However, if you answered, "We're not very good at that," to most or all of the questions, then you probably have a culture problem.

Another quick test for cultural health is to consider how often you hear people say, "That's not my job." Think about it. Do you hear that phrase a lot at your company? If people are communicating and collaborating, if they trust their leadership and own their work, and if the mission of the company lines up with their values, then all employees feel like part owners and take ownership for the responsibilities, successes, and failures that come with business ownership. They feel like their organization matters to them, instead of maintaining a "that's not my job" attitude.

Yes, people will say this from time to time, but there will be a good reason behind it. For example, if we're closing out the second quarter and our financial people are running around trying to get everything done, and someone asks them to help with the party planning for the Fourth of July, they won't be too eager to help out. That's okay. However, if many people in your organization are often saying, "That's not my job," you can bet there's a problem. Just as the Golden Rule is a litmus test for gauging behavior in a healthy culture, the frequency with which you hear people saying something isn't their job is a litmus test for an unhealthy one.

What to Do When There's a Toxic Culture

You can attack each of the areas addressed in these questions individually, and that will work well if your culture is slightly off-track. However, if after answering these questions, you realize you have a serious problem and a potentially toxic culture—one that prevents your people from enjoying their work—then you have to take more direct and dramatic action.

You have three options for making a radical shift in the culture. First, you can shift people around in their roles. You may have simply put people in positions they're not happy in or not good at, and they need to be moved. For example, you may have people with excellent technical skills but no project management or people management experience, yet they were promoted into management positions. They don't have the skill set to be proactive, manage a lot of moving pieces, hit deadlines, or supervise and lead a team, and so you may have to put them into other positions where they can succeed with the skills they have.

The second option is to examine the culture of the people at the top, and if there's a problem, let them know they have to make a change. If that's you, then you may have to take a hard look at your own behaviors. You can't go through the motions of naming the full set of culture values for your company, then act out a completely different set of values, and expect a healthy culture to manifest itself. That's like building a really cool car body and throwing a cheap engine in it. It may look pretty on the outside, but it won't run well.

Don't overlook your responsibility in this. You may not feel your actions are important, but, as you are a leader, people watch you and emulate your behavior. The actions and behaviors of the leadership at your company can set the groundwork for building a unique culture and an irresistible workplace.

If you're not in a leadership position but instead are an employee of a company with a toxic culture, then your best option may be to leave. I'm not encouraging anyone to job-hop, but if you're stuck in an organization where the people at the top are not exhibiting a healthy culture, nor do they plan to change, don't expect to be the sole agent of culture change. Change from the bottom is very difficult to accomplish. If you have the ear of someone at the top who is willing to accept your recommendations and take positive action, it can happen, but that's not how it usually works out.

Culture is identified from the bottom—from the people within your organization—but it cannot survive if it's not replicated and reinforced from the very top. For example, one of our people, Holly Tate (mentioned earlier), who has worked with us on culture from the very beginning, tells people all the time that our culture wouldn't work if I weren't committed to cultivating it and living it out. None of my team expects perfection from me (which is good, because I'm far from perfect). But they do expect me to show consistent effort to reinforce our culture.

The third and most radical option is to fire someone—likely someone at or near the top of the organization. No matter how successful your company is, a bad culture can cause irreparable damage, and sometimes the only way to ward off a downward spiral is to remove the people who are introducing toxicity into the culture. For example, Uber, once everybody's darling as the biggest fund-raiser in US history and with a valuation higher than General Motors,[23] is now known for its former CEO's being a jerk to one of his drivers. The company put that CEO, Travis Kalanick, on a three-month mandatory sabbatical while it assessed what to do with him because of his conduct, and now he's gone.[24]

I wrote an article for *Forbes* about why United Airlines will survive its crisis after dragging a man off a plane and why Uber won't survive its current crisis.[25] I received a tremendous amount of feedback on that article from people who agreed: If you have a toxic culture and make a sincere attempt to change it, you can save your company. But if you allow a toxic culture to fester, you put your entire company at risk—no matter how big it is.

When you look at our unfair advantage as a faith-based organization and look at two of the arguably largest corporate disruptors in the past twenty years—Enron and Uber—you can see that if you don't have a healthy culture, you don't have anything. Before you set specific culture values for your company, make sure your foundation—the cultural values of the people at the top—is healthy.

CHAPTER 3

Our Kind of Crazy

WHEN MY FIRM STARTED winning company culture awards, we reverse-engineered our development, asking ourselves what we did—and are still doing—that makes us who we are. What makes our company unique and defines "our kind of crazy"? How did we get here?

I thought about how I spent the bulk of my time and realized it was conducting interviews with people who wanted to work here. My main goal was never to convince them to work for me. Rather, I tried to talk them out of it. I let them know up front that Vanderbloemen Search Group had a particular kind of "crazy" and might not be the best fit for them. That's not a slick, passive-aggressive or reverse-psychology sales tactic. I wanted them to know we have a distinct culture, and if it wasn't for them, they'd be miserable. On the other hand, if it is their kind of crazy, they'd probably be successful and enjoy the work.

It's not that there are places with intrinsically better work environments than others, but rather, each workplace is different, with its own kind of crazy. The key is staffing your business with people who share those qualities that make your organization unique—whatever they are. Once you understand what makes your company culture different and you can describe it, you can verbalize your culture to candidates in your interviewing process so there are no surprises for them and fewer bad hires for you. For example, I tell interviewees, "If you want steady, predictable work, with a day-in and day-out, ordinary routine, then this position won't work for you. If you leave here today thinking, 'Man, they are all so weird,' you're right. We are a little weird, but so is every company, in its own way. If our kind of crazy isn't for you, that's fine—there's another company out there that's probably a better fit."

This approach has led to high success rates in hiring, because we get people who can be happy and successful with our kind of crazy. There are no surprises and no disappointments. The hiring stage is the most critical time and the best tool you have for creating a healthy culture, so you have to be able to figure out whether somebody is a good fit or not.

Being upfront about your company's culture can prevent you from making mistakes. For example, a highly talented young man applied for a controller position at my company. I thought the interviews went well, and he certainly checked off the "competency box." I spent the interview telling him what our culture was like and why it wasn't for everyone. We agreed to move forward with a second interview. More positive vibes came from that, but I also used it as a chance to underline how important (and strange) our culture was. We decided to offer him the job, but he called and said, "I think I'm going to back out." It wasn't the position, the location, the hours, or the pay. He just didn't love the culture at our company. And I'm so glad he backed out. No matter how competent people are, if they don't fit our culture, they will end up hurting our company.

Every person at your company influences every other person somehow, and so hiring someone who didn't fit our culture, and who wouldn't have been happy, would have had an adverse effect on every individual and every team in some way. That effect may be small, or it could be dramatic, but you have the opportunity to prevent it when you hire people. Every time you hire someone, think about how that person can strengthen the team or weaken it. You'll have more solid teams if you hire around culture.

Finding Your Culture

To get to that point, you have to figure out what your own kind of crazy is. What makes your organization unique? You need to know this so you can communicate it to potential new hires and for other reasons. At Vanderbloemen Search Group, we began to define our kind of crazy with a mission statement focused on values. Many companies have ninety-day plans, annual plans, and multiyear strategic plans focused on products, services, technologies, and finances, but how many of them ever make it a point to sit down and discuss the *kind* of company they want to be? What kind of people, behaviors, and activities reflect your company?

When we were developing our mission statement, we started with what our culture already was. While I was figuring out what made our company unique and successful, I stumbled upon a great question. I haven't heard it anywhere else but have used it since then to help organizations figure out their culture. I looked at our team and asked them, "*When we're functioning at our very best, what do we do that's common to our organization but uncommon in traditional companies?*" In other words, "What is our kind of crazy?" Answering those questions helped us identify our uniqueness—our specific kind of crazy.

Ten of us sat down—that was the whole company. Three of the people involved were very new, and in fact, it was the first day of work for two of them. This conversation was so important to establish who we were, and the kind of company we would become, and I wanted everyone involved in the conversation.

Identifying your own kind of crazy takes time. From when we first sat down to discuss what kind of crazy we were as individuals, teams, and as a company when we're functioning at our best, to when we actually wrote our mission statement, was a six-month process, and we were a small company at the time.

As a start-up, our small size and limited time in business were advantages. The bigger the company and the longer it has been in business, the more entrenched people are in current culture, and the longer this process takes. But no matter how long your company has been around or how many people work there, once you've identified your kind of crazy, embedded it, and committed to it, you'll start to change the way you do everything.

Here's an example of what I mean about a company's particular kind of crazy. Google is open with its employees about its finances. It tells them everything. This seems kind of crazy, but its vision statement and mission statement say it wants "to organize the world's information and make it universally accessible and useful."[26] How could Google have a culture in which it doesn't talk about finances with that mission statement?

You can figure out your existing culture, and what your people want the culture to be, through internal surveys, input, and feedback. As we established particular traits that identified my company's culture, we wrote them on oversized Post-it notes and hung them on the walls. We weren't telling everyone who we were, but who we thought we were—and we were asking for feedback. People started writing what they thought about these ideas right on the Post-its, and then they started adding their own. This way, all employees had an opportunity to take part in a brainstorming session about our company's culture as ideas occurred to them, instead of in a formal meeting or, worse, by reading something leadership was dictating to them. We needed to decide who we were and who we wanted to become as a company, and so our mission evolved into a vision, too.

There's a lot of old-school thinking about vision. One school of thought says the leader's role is to find the vision for the company: Go off on vacation, on a personal retreat, or as my pastor friends would say, "Go off to the mountain and come back down with two stone tablets with all the values written down, Ten Commandments style. If you can't define the vision, you're not a leader."

But over the years, I'm learning that isn't the way it works. My process taught me that the two stone tablets aren't received from the Divine at the top of Mount Sinai (or any mountain). The stone tablets with your company culture are at the *bottom* of the mountain. The values you're looking for are embedded in your people. It's your job to figure out what those values are and work with your people to articulate them.

After everyone had a chance to write their comments and ideas on the giant Post-its, we all sat down, as a company, to discuss them. I wanted my people to explain their thoughts: how they contributed to our company's culture and to its success. I also wanted to know why they believed what we did was different than what most other companies did.

I let that sit for a long time, partly by accident. We got really busy, and I didn't have time to deal with it. But looking back, taking that time was the best approach. Sometimes, taking time away from a topic—even a day—allows the ideas presented around it to "gel," so you have a better understanding of how those ideas are connected. As my mother has told me for years, "Chili always tastes better after sitting in the refrigerator for a few days after you cook it."

After several months, we talked about culture and the ideas we had generated and came up with "buckets" in which to group ideas with common themes. It was the start of our six-month journey toward defining our cultural values, and those became part of our mission. Those values came from within the company and were culled from the people who spent every day doing the work that made us successful—and unique. I didn't have to climb a mountain or go on a retreat to discover who my people were; the answer was within them, and they needed a forum in which to share it. Giant Post-it notes and company-wide brainstorming sessions may not be your kind of crazy for writing a mission statement, but it worked for us.

Once you know your kind of crazy, you'll do things that may appear nontraditional in a corporate culture; yet those actions won't be crazy for you, because they directly correlate with who you've decided you are and say you are.

<u>OUR VALUES</u>

At Vanderbloemen Search Group, nine values guide our team culture. Visit vanderbloemen.com/about to learn more.

- Broadband Love—We're a company built on the values of our Christian faith. As a company, we endeavor to live in grace and walk in love. We strive to show love to each client and candidate with whom we interact.

- Unusual Servanthood—We exist to serve our clients and candidates in a way that makes them say, "I've never been treated like that by a company."

- Wow-Making Excellence—We can't promise to be all things to all people, but we can strive to be all things to our clients. We endeavor to underpromise and overdeliver through each step of the search process. We also work to be a thought leader in the search industry, creating top-notch articles and resources to help organizations follow staffing and leadership best practices.

- Ridiculous Responsiveness—In the world of smartphones, the world is at our fingertips. Quality comes first, but speed comes next. We want to deliver quality service at lightning speed.

- Solution-Side Living—The Vanderbloemen team members are problem solvers, always having a solution mentality and not a victim mentality.

- Ever-Increasing Agility—Being flexible is too rigid. We strive for agility to serve our clients and candidates with excellence in an ever-changing marketplace. Each employee at Vanderbloemen has "other duties as required" built into his or her job description.

- Stewardship of Life—We measure success on our ability to maintain personal and corporate financial, spiritual, physical, and vocational boundaries. Each employee is required to charitably give of his or her time, talent, and resources.

- Constant Improvement—Vanderbloemen strives for kaizen, the Japanese business philosophy of continuous improvement of working practices and personal efficiency. Each

Vanderbloemen employee has an insatiable curiosity for making systems and processes better. The marketplace is changing daily, and Vanderbloemen strives to stay ahead of the curve by constantly asking, "How can we improve?"

- Contagious Fun—We take our work seriously but not ourselves. We love what we do, and our joy in helping our clients is contagious. You'll often find us at a local restaurant enjoying one another's company after work hours, because we genuinely like one another.

Rick Holliday, executive director of ministry services, and Andy Stanley, senior pastor, lead one of the largest churches in the country, North Point Ministries, in Georgia. They're known for having a strong leadership culture. About five years ago, while they were experiencing high growth, they realized something. Rick told me, "We've grown from six to six hundred employees over twenty years, and we've just been assuming everyone knows what our values are. We need to go through the process of articulating exactly what our cultural values are."

Now, Andy Stanley is arguably one of the most visionary and articulate pastors in the country, and perhaps *the* best communicator in the American Church today. No one can turn a phrase like Andy. Pastors listen to his podcast by the tens of thousands, and people hang on his every word. An artfully crafted document defining North Point Ministries' cultural values would have been an easy task for Andy. But the church knew that wasn't what they needed—the cultural values had to come from someplace else.

The church leaders didn't say, "Andy, go figure out our values, then come back and tell us what they are, because you're the senior pastor and you can say it cooler than we can." Instead, they decided to take the time necessary to uncover the church's values at the bottom of the mountain. This made much more sense than sending Andy off to write them himself on a couple of stone tablets—or a mission statement written on a web page.

Of course, having a pastor write a church's values would save a lot of time and money in the short term, and North Point isn't frivolous in its spending. The leadership is financially savvy and aware of the cost of holding a meeting. It doesn't take much to break down each person's salary to cost per hour, add all those costs up, and multiply the result by the number of hours spent on a project. Taking the long and slow approach to determining your values—and your kind of crazy—is *not* without cost. However, the cost of identifying, defining, and articulating an organization's values pays big dividends in the long term. Likewise, the cost of not doing it can be enormous.

North Point Ministries took a whole *year* to go through the process of sending out surveys, bringing leaders together to look at the responses, and collaborating to determine the church's values. Questions and comments went up and down the pipeline between the employees, management, and senior leadership. For a church that size, that's exactly how it needed to be done.

Melissa Allen, as mentioned previously, is the CEO and co-owner of GetUWired. When it started working on its culture,

it was a small company generating under $1 million a year. Melissa decided to shut the doors for three days, a move that cost the company $170,000 in lost revenue and paid-out salaries. She used this time to bring the employees in to define the company's culture. Those meetings gave people a voice, and so they not only spoke about it and contributed their thoughts and ideas, but they also bought into the final definition of that culture and took ownership of it. Since then, GetUWired's culture has been a hinge point of its success. Staff stay longer there than at most companies. The company's vision is clearer than ever. And it has experienced more growth than it ever expected. Melissa says there is a straight line from the current success back to the work everyone did codifying the culture.

Our Culture

Those early meetings I had with my staff about our company's culture uncovered surprising information about how we acted and reacted. While Vanderbloemen Search Group embodies the positive side of all the questions in this chapter, representing a healthy culture, two unusual traits in particular stood out as unique and a bit crazy. These behaviors were how we worked when we were at our best, and while they seemed crazy, they were definitely an important part of our company's culture. We incorporated them into our mission statement.

Ridiculous Responsiveness

When I started the company, I was on my own. My wife offered to help me out by sending a bill to my first client, if I ever got one. That's how a new business starts, though—often with no or few clients.

Whenever someone emailed, called, or simply mentioned in passing, "I was thinking of using you," I was *very* quick to respond. I heard over and over, "Wow, it's amazing how quickly you got back to us." It's amazing how much your response time improves when you realize that if you don't land a client, your family doesn't eat. But beyond sheer survival instinct, my intuition told me I needed to keep responding quickly. People appreciated it and, apparently, a lot of other people weren't doing it. People respond to speed. In business, speed wins. In lieu of a real mission statement, "ridiculous responsiveness" became my ad hoc motto.

Once I had turned my one-man show into a full-fledged company with clients, I started hiring people who responded rapidly to my interview offers. They seemed to be almost obsessive-compulsive about getting back to me quickly. I knew fast responses got me clients, and I wanted the people who worked for me to have that same sense of urgency.

Later, I read a study about inbound marketing and response times. Inbound marketing includes activities focused on customers reaching out to a company, rather than the company reaching out to customers, such as when you fill out an online form allowing a company to contact you about a product or service. You usually give your name and email address, and you might answer a few questions about your needs, then it's on the company to respond to you. The study showed that the basic purpose of a sales conversation is not to close the sale but to have the next sales conversation. It's actually very unusual to close a deal right away, or during that initial interaction. The study found that when someone fills out an online form, and a company gets back to them within sixty seconds—and does so without using some automated reply but a *real*, human response—the chances of the company having another conversation with that person is in the upper 90th percentile. If the company waits twenty-four hours, *one* day, the chances drop to less than 1 percent. The article also said the average response time for small businesses that use inbound marketing is forty-two hours.[27]

We didn't realize the accuracy of what we kept saying—that speed wins—but the study verified it. Being ridiculously responsive wins. We do things fast. We get back to people. We took that value and found an alliterative, "sticky" way to say it, and it stuck!

Cultural values can't be plain-vanilla concepts that have no basis in who you are and what you do. They have to reflect your reality. They have to be real. You can't say something like, "Excellence, that's our value," because who values mediocrity? You also can't just say you're responsive, because every company responds to its customers eventually. Ridiculous responsiveness *means* something to people. You can put a pin in it and hang it on the wall, and people know exactly what you're talking about. In fact, we have the phrase "ridiculous responsiveness" hanging in our conference room, along with our other values. The letters are giant stickers, so if our values change or are refined over the years, we can peel them off and tweak them, or replace them. Sometimes a company's values, and its culture, change over time. Remember, those things come from the people and aren't etched in stone.

Wow-Making Excellence

As noted above, it doesn't make sense to make excellence a value, because probably no one values mediocrity. No company strives for mediocrity, yet I've lost count of the number of companies that use excellence as a value. That's not a cultural value for us any more than keeping the lights on is. We sought to amplify our values so they described *us*—not every other company. We wanted the values to articulate *our* kind of crazy.

Our team, in deciding our values, talked about the times when our excellence was so over the top that our clients said, "Wow!" We wanted to continue making them respond this way, so that became our standard: wow-making excellence.

Actually, our clients weren't the first to respond that way. Rather, we were hearing "wow" from the strangest of places: Our number-one referral source for new business was people we'd interviewed but had *not* hired. When they talked to other prospective employers, our name came up. "You should call the people at Vanderbloemen," they would say. "They didn't hire me, but—wow—they really took care of me and didn't treat me like a number. If you really want to fill this position, you should give them a call." Our clients are employers who hire us to help them find people for their staff, and people who interviewed with us were telling those companies to contact us. That's when you know you have top-tier excellence—when other people are saying "wow" about what you're doing.

When we had nine values as a team, and we needed one more to make an even ten, I got stuck. It was making me crazy that we had only nine values. The day came when we would present the final one—a six-month process of wordsmithing—and I had nothing. As I sat at breakfast that morning with the youngest of my seven children, my two-year-old daughter, she looked at me and said, "Today, I will not drama."

She was right about the importance of lack of drama. My people don't bring drama into the workplace, and that's contributed to our culture and success. There's enough of it inherent in the work, in people's personal lives, and in the world we live in, so there's no reason to bring it into the day-to-day interactions in the workplace. As much as I was tempted to add that value—no drama—and round out the list of values to an even ten, it wasn't part of our crowdsourced process, and so I chose to honor the process and not add it.

You don't have to have ten values. Our number of values changes as our company changes, and we consider what's important and what makes us successful and unique.

Your Values and Those of Your Clients

Our group is not specific to one particular part of Christian faith, and we serve a wide range of value-driven organizations, not just churches. There are businesses that share our values, although they aren't specifically churches. They may be companies run by people with a faith-based background who need our help to find them a CFO. We enjoy serving those who have similar values.

To some degree, all values are faith-based values. Our group tries to err on the side of loving people more and judging less. Some of our clients might look at our whole client list and say our clients are too conservative or too liberal—too this or too that. But judging our clients isn't our job. Our job is to love and serve our clients well and to serve them in an unusual way.

An ideal business relationship is one between organizations that share the same values, but again, you have to be agile. Not every business you work with, or every client you serve, will share your culture, but as long as you don't abandon your core values, you can adapt.

The first year my business took off, I got *way* out of shape. I traveled a lot and I'm a foodie, so I enjoyed the local cuisine *a lot*. When I was in Tennessee, I ate ribs. When I was in Maryland, I ate crab cakes. When I was in North Carolina, I ate barbecue. It was all delicious, but I gained thirty-five pounds in the process. My health took a further beating because I was trying to grab naps on planes instead of sleeping at night. Between the food and the schedule, the job would have killed me if I didn't include healthy choices in my day.

As a result, I started hiring people who shared my health-focused interests, and health and fitness have become an important part of our culture. In fact, our first fitness challenge was one of the closest experiences we've shared as a team. Working at our company doesn't mean people have to be superfit or look a certain way. But it does mean that you have to be committed to living a life that balances your mental, physical, and spiritual lives. The first year we did a fitness challenge together, people bonded as they posted pictures of food, workouts, or their sleep schedule. As we worked out together (with a wide variance in intensities), the team came together. One person said, "The team that sweats together stays together," and that seemed to be true for us. Living out that value—a value that may appear to have nothing to do with business—actually improved our sense of teamwork. I believe it also made us better at our work.

Culture at Other Companies

Connexus Community Church in Toronto isn't part of the Bible Belt. Generally speaking, it can be difficult to bring people into church who haven't already committed to attending, so Connexus uses creative methods to attract people.

The pastor there, Carey Nieuwhof, understands that his church, like many organizations, wants to be perfect at everything it does. However, striving for perfection can become a problem. You can get to the point where, if what you're doing isn't perfect, you give up and decide not to do it at all. I spoke with Carey, and he told me he manages this problem by, settling for something a lot more realistic than perfection. He says, "Battle mediocrity."[28]

No one can be perfect at everything, but everyone can battle mediocrity. You can spend ten hours making something 20 percent better, or you can spend one hundred hours making something 2 percent better. Spending one hundred hours for such a small return isn't a good use of your resources, and when you strive for perfection, you run the risk of alienating some of the people you're trying to help. Even if you do achieve perfection, your employees, clients, and the organizations you work with probably won't, and you need to meet them where they are.

What Counts in Culture and What Doesn't

When you're defining your values, you have to go beyond the minimum expectations of human decency and workplace professionalism. For example, "Respect one another" is not a cultural value. "Show up on time to work" isn't a cultural value either. Those behaviors are expected of anyone at work, no matter what the culture is like, so you should be more specific and, of course, have higher expectations for yourself and your staff. Vague, meaningless cultural values lead to a vague, meaningless culture.

Having a tight culture doesn't mean having a place where everyone is identical. There is a book written about HubSpot called *Disrupted: My Misadventure in the Start-Up Bubble*.[29] Basically, a baby boomer got a job at the company and wrote a book about his experience.[30] He claimed he was treated differently there because he wasn't a millennial. HubSpot caught some heat over the book and said the guy wasn't on the level when he took the job; the company believed he was working there with the intention of gathering material for a book, although he claims that was not the case.

Regardless, the experience caused HubSpot to take a closer look at its environment. It realized all of its employees were young, white millennials. It had overlooked the lack of diversity in its workforce and had hired a lot of people who were all very similar. The goal of creating a healthy culture isn't to hire people of the same gender, race, or age, but to hire people who are a good cultural fit. HubSpot has since made changes to its workforce, but it hasn't changed its cultural values.

When everyone at the office looks the same and acts the same way, and everyone orders the same thing off the same menu, that's not culture. Culture goes much deeper. HubSpot has won numerous awards for being the best place to work in Boston,[31] and so the release of *Disrupted* blindsided the leadership. They couldn't laugh it off. Instead, HubSpot took a step back and said, "Wow, we really are all young, white millennials, and we need to step up our game in diversity. All of us looking alike—that's not a cultural value."

New Versus Established Organizations

Young companies and older, more established organizations will have very different cultures. In a new organization or a start-up company, the culture is tied to the top five people. In older organizations, the culture has become entrenched over the years, and the people who set it originally may not even be working there anymore.

When I went to First Presbyterian in Houston, I wanted to change the culture, regardless of who the top five people were. The church has been there since Sam Houston's time, and the culture was established long ago, so it was very difficult to make changes. At a brand-new organization, influencing the top five people is easier, and doing so can change the entire culture of a company very quickly.

Think of this as shifting directions in the water. If you're in a young company, shifting can be like turning a sailboat. It's not hard. But if you're in a company that's been around for multiple generations, and perhaps hundreds of years, and the culture hasn't changed much, you're turning an aircraft carrier—and that's a lot harder.

Codifying Culture

To codify your culture, make some of your value phrases sticky. They should be memorable. Everyone remembers the phrase "ridiculous responsiveness." In fact, I belong to a group of about six hundred high-growth-company CEOs, the Oxford Center for Entrepreneurs (https://oxfordcenter.com), and since I've talked about cultural values to that group, I've seen the term "ridiculous responsiveness" show up on the websites of several of the members. Imitation is the highest form of flattery, but it was copied because the term was sticky.

Once you and your staff have established your culture, you have to document it somehow. You codify your culture by writing it, and it doesn't have to be on paper. For example, Netflix has an online culture deck with close to a hundred slides.[32]

Once you've documented your values, you have to live them. You need to find ways to start living out the culture you've defined in every phase of the organization. Companies winning at culture have made it more than a poster on a wall, words on white paper, or a presentation slide deck. They spread culture and make it a living, breathing part of every phase of an employee's life cycle. We'll talk about how to spread culture throughout your company and prevent culture "leaks" in section II, "Great Teams Spread Culture," and how to ensure it's lived out throughout your employees' life cycle in section III, "Culture Permeates the Employee Life Cycle."

GREAT TEAMS
SPREAD CULTURE

CHAPTER 4

Great Culture, Top to Bottom

E VERY COMPANY I'VE STUDIED that has a great culture has a leader living that culture who's totally committed to it. Many of them pose questions to themselves regularly about what they're doing to maintain a healthy culture. They also tend to formalize this to ensure it gets done.

When I spoke with Terry Nawrot, the COO at Informz, an email marketing solutions provider, he told me his company posts its values in the building, but spreading culture also demands a lot of one-on-one communication. At Informz, the CEO and the COO meet with every employee once a year. Even though it isn't a huge organization, that commitment takes a lot of time. In addition, managers have one-on-one meetings with team members twice a month. They also do "shout-outs," saying "thank you" and "good job" to the people living out the cultural values and not just hitting their numbers. As they've driven cultural values throughout their organization, the complaint levels have gone down and positive feedback has gone up. Terry said they also do things most other companies do to show their appreciation, like give employees pizza and bagels to thank them for adopting a healthy culture and living it.

If you're hiring the right people, you've defined the culture with your people, and you've codified it and spread it throughout your organization, you're more likely to see people living that culture early on and without being asked or reminded. For example, at my firm, we prepare packets that talk about our business, and we use them for talks with potential candidates. During our robust seasons, there's a lot to do, and everyone stays extremely busy. On one occasion, a consultant asked if he could have an extra one. That may seem like a minor request, but it's actually a lot of work to put one of them together, and the person in charge of the packets had been with us two weeks. Considering his workload, and with his being new to the job, I figured adding one more thing to his plate would put him over the top. Instead, he jumped right in and offered to get it done. When I see people proactively going beyond their job description in an effort to help their coworkers, their team, the company, and our clients, I see our culture at work.

That attitude has to exist at every level. Leaders have to embody it. Spreading culture is easier with a smaller, flatter organization with fewer layers, but regardless of the size of an organization or how it's structured, everyone has to be on board with the culture. There can't be an "us and them," or a different set of rules for employees and management.

Learning by Example

The more the leader lives out the culture, the more employees will follow suit. If the leader embodies, pushes, and champions culture, participates with the employees, and is visible and accessible, the culture will thrive.

Before I started interviewing CEOs and asking questions about how other companies develop and maintain a healthy culture, I thought I was doing a decent job living out culture at my own firm. The more I learned, the more challenged I felt to live out our culture with intention. It's up to the leader of an organization to set the tone for the rest of the company. If you're a team leader, look in the mirror and ask yourself how you're living out your culture. Take it on as a personal challenge.

I'm reminded of the comparison of two generals. The first general sat in the back of his army, while the second general was on the front line checking in with his soldiers every day. Who do you think the soldiers were loyal to?

Living out your company's values should feel natural. It shouldn't feel unnatural or forced, and if it's not natural, then either the values are wrong or you, as the leader, are wrong for the company. If the leader doesn't match the cultural values, one of those two things is out of place.

Losing Culture

The team at Google said, "We have a very healthy amount of paranoia about losing our culture, and it keeps it on track."[33]

Losing culture is something I'm afraid of on a daily basis. As my company grows, I worry about it even more because it's harder to maintain a healthy culture as you add more people. It's easy to end up with silos of people who develop their own culture, and it may not be in line with the culture of your company.

I started my firm on a card table, and as we grew, we moved into a horrible space with paper-thin walls. We were practically on top of each other, and everyone could hear what everyone else was doing, but we also communicated easily and everyone knew what everyone else was doing.

Then we moved to a bigger building and went from one thousand square feet to five thousand square feet. It was still pretty tight, but it was the best we could afford. The desks were crammed together in close quarters, and there was really no privacy at all. One of our interns at that place went the entire summer without using the bathroom at work for fear his coworkers would hear him.

You'd think we would've wanted nothing more than to get out of that tiny space. But when we moved to a professional building—going from five thousand to fifteen thousand square feet, with a corner that wrapped around the core of the building—we weren't completely excited. The first thing we noticed was that we couldn't all see one another. There were sections within the office. I thought, *We're going to turn into silos. What are we going to do?* I was scared to death.

Whenever there's a threat to the culture, such as moving into a new space, you have to be aware of it and proactive about it. Communication and collaboration aren't going to happen if people are divided, so you have to come up with new ways to ensure they're working together. Each time we've grown, so have my concerns; therefore, I'm very aware of our physical space and how it affects our culture.

Physical Space and Culture

When we moved to the bigger office, we knew we'd need to be intentional about designing the space in a way that matched our culture. That didn't mean we were going to put in a Ms. Pac-Man machine, but we did create a workspace that promoted collaboration. Later, I discovered this is what the book *The Best Place to Work* recommends to build a great culture.[34]

We moved thirty people from five thousand to fifteen thousand square feet, tripling our floor space, and we finally had room to spread out. We bought some big chairs from IKEA so everyone would be comfortable. Frankly, this was the first office where we could even fit chairs like that.

The best space in the office had a wonderful view of the city. Rather than make it my private office, we made it the break room. I realized the room would traditionally be the CEO's space, but it didn't make sense to keep it to myself.

The architect told us the break room was way too big and we'd be wasting space, but we knew, with our culture, we'd use it. People eat together in the break room every single day. If they go out, they get their food to go and bring it back to the office so they can sit together there. It's not a dirty, ugly, avoid-at-all-costs kitchenette with burnt-coffee smells and microwaved Hot Pockets. Our break room is big and airy and a place where people like to gather for eating, for meetings, or to talk. In addition to the break room, we put "huddle spots" throughout the office so people can collaborate and communicate. Having designated areas for these casual, formal, and impromptu activities encourages the culture we've developed and decreases the odds of silos developing in isolated areas. Silos can create their own culture, which may not be in line with the company's and may actually even contradict the healthy one.

We reserved the second large office for our administrators. This is the absolute opposite of what conventional wisdom would have told us to do, but those team members work together a lot, and they need a space to talk. They also need to feel good about where they are.

In *The Best Place to Work*, Friedman notes, "Something's deeply wrong with the design of a workplace when the only way for an employee to feel productive is to physically leave the building."[35] We wanted everyone to feel productive at work, and we achieved that without spending a lot of money. The total cost of the build-out of the space to suit our needs was about $61 per square foot, including all the wiring, computer cabling, audiovisual setup, graphics—everything—which is unheard of. By comparison, grocery stores pay around $100 per square foot. We wanted simple and inexpensive, but we also wanted to create a place where people would feel safe. We have a lot of teams where men and women work together, and we have high ethical standards.

We decided to put glass most of the way around every office. I didn't want anyone to see a closed door and wonder what was going on behind it. The visibility the glass allows complements the visibility of our culture and allows people to work together free of worry or suspicion.

For private phone calls, we have phone booths set up around the office with an iPad outside each one so you can check the availability and schedule time in them. In keeping with our mission as a faith-based organization that serves churches, we call these Confessional #1, Confessional #2, and so forth. We also have small conference rooms, so people who don't have an office can still have a quiet space for meetings and interviews. The seven dedicated offices are reserved for team leaders, so they can have space to meet with their staff, individually or as a team. The setup and design of the office space fosters communication and collaboration, but it also creates accountability. It's pretty hard to play video games on a computer all day with this kind of environment. Sitting at my desk, I'm able to smile and wave at everyone in the office as they pass by, and that open interaction creates a friendly atmosphere.

We're a modest company, and we place more importance on people and values than things. We wanted that to be evident in our decor, so rather than investing in a lot of artwork for the walls, we set the tone right away by hanging our values around the office. We put in a bunch of TVs, which aren't expensive these days, and we play a carousel of pictures on them around our company's culture.

As a search group, we host coaching seminars, and companies send their staff to these seminars for several days. We want them to have a friendly, positive space where they can get to know us and our company. When potential clients visit us in our office, the conversion rate is astounding. Most of them want to work with us, and when I ask them why, they almost always mention the culture. They can feel it in our office, and they know it's not just something we win awards for or write about.

Although he's not part of the workplace setup, we have a character in our office who adds to the culture of our environment: our CCO, or chief canine officer, Moses. When I started the firm, having a dog around wasn't a big deal, but as we moved into bigger offices I had to insist that allowing him in the building be written into the lease, along with any future successors. We know every mascot is temporary, and Moses is an interim CCO, and we have to take that into consideration in our succession planning. He's important to our culture and an instant icebreaker. If someone comes into my office and I'm on a call, he or she can visit with Moses until I'm available, and it creates a friendly mood. He's not just the CCO; Moses is the framily pet.

Virtual Culture

Remote workforces, in which people work from geographically distant locations and often from their home offices, are becoming more popular. The work at my company demands a lot of collaborative problem solving, which is very difficult for a team to accomplish without being together physically, no matter how good you think technology is. That doesn't mean if you're working in a virtual setting, you can't have a healthy culture.

Bryan Miles of BELAY has a workforce of around six hundred people who are all virtually connected. His staff includes full-time and part-time employees plus independent contractors, and he drives his cultural values across the internet.

The company has regular, virtual conference calls with the whole team. He once brought a new employee in to talk about her hopes and dreams for joining the company, and she talked about how she wanted so badly to be a part of their culture. Bryan thought, *Wow, we can have a culture and not be in the same room. A virtual workforce can work really well when I lead by example.* Now the team talks about culture on these calls. Bryan says when you get the right kind of people together—people who are committed to the same values and culture—the virtual environment works.

I asked him about the return on investment (ROI) on his virtual environment and the culture developed at BELAY. He responded, "The ROI is when I hear my people say, 'I'm ruined for life. I'll never go to work anywhere else.'"

Of course, not every culture is a good fit for every employee, and you can have people working for you who don't like the culture. However, the majority of your employees—if they've been involved in its development or have been hired with culture in mind—will enjoy being part of the framily at your company, and they'll guard and protect the culture. Protecting your culture has to be an ongoing process or it will leak, but there are ways to ensure your culture remains intact.

CHAPTER 5

Stop Culture Leaks

W HEN WE WON THE Best Places to Work award, I was amazed the award didn't go to some cool start-up you'd see on the cover of *Fast Company* or *Inc*. We're a group of ordinary people working together with a common mission. Before coming together at Vanderbloemen Search Group, many of us worked in churches, which aren't known for their innovation. We're made up of a lot of millennials, who are new to their career, and we try to help value-based companies—and in large part, churches—find a pastor. That doesn't seem like the ideal breeding ground for developing a thriving company culture. However, our shared values and culture have brought us together in a healthy working relationship in which we treat one another like friends or family, like framily.

As thrilled as I was seeing my company recognized this way, I was instantly worried as well. "Oh wow, we won" quickly turned to, "Oh man, we'd better work hard or we might lose it." I was captured by some level of fear. I wondered how long our culture would last—was worried it would go away.

If you're leading a start-up company, you can do a lot of research about building a great culture, starting with this book. What you'll discover is, for the most part, building a healthy culture isn't complicated if you're leading from the gut. I didn't have a roadmap when I started, and most of what we've done, we did because it felt right. At the time, we didn't know if it was "*the* right way" to do it, but the more research I did and the more people I talked with at other companies, the more I realized that doing what felt right was the right way to create an irresistible workplace.

One hunch I had that turned out to be true was around my concern with protecting our values, especially as we added more people. I knew the bigger we got, the harder it would be to hang on to our values and spread our culture throughout the growing company. I know I've said this before, but it's something you need to remember—big companies have very little chance of beating small companies when it comes to culture. If you look at the raw scores from the surveys on best places to work, they are usually divided into groups: 10 to 50 employees, 50 to 100, 100 to 250, 250 to 500, and so forth. All employees take the same test. All the tests use the same scoring system. When you compare the scores between surveys, they are very similar. The largest-company category doesn't come close to beating out the medium or small companies in the categories of culture or best places to work or in *anything* that measures satisfaction with the workplace, for that matter. These indexes have questions such as, "Do I like coming here? Would I refer a friend?" Generally speaking, the bigger the company, the lower the score.

You see, the bigger your company gets, the more opportunities there are for culture leaks. Most business leaders want their business to grow and grow fast, but the faster you grow and the more people you hire, the harder it will be to maintain your culture and values. As our group continues to grow, I've become hell-bent on maintaining our heavenly culture—a culture we love.

According to *Houston Business Journal's* Best Places to Work, between 2015 to 2016 (when our headcount grew), our company went from the sixth to the third best place to work in the city in our company-size division.

We were the *only* company in the small-business division that both grew in headcount and rose in ranking—and our raw score went up. I intend to maintain that upward trend as long as we're in the small-business category. I want to see us rise from third to second place, then second to first. A continuous rise in rankings shows you can build, protect, and improve a company's culture even as you grow.

I want our business to keep growing. I want to make an impact on the world by helping churches and other organizations build their own roadmap to an irresistible workplace. In order to do that, I've come to realize we have to be willing to spend more money on culture. We have to put a larger percentage of our budget and time into it for it to work.

I'd challenge other business owners and team leaders reading this book to try to prove me wrong: If you can grow your team and improve your culture at the same time, you'll never have a hiring problem, and you likely won't have a retention problem either. People will want to work for you, and they'll want to continue working for you.

You can grow *and* improve your culture, but you have to be intentional about it, making sure everyone is on board with your company's values. You also have to proactively safeguard your business against potentially destructive culture leaks.

Culture Leaks

Imagine you have a pipeline in your backyard. If that pipeline gets a leak, you can probably plug it with one hand. If there's another leak, you can plug it with your other hand. Now imagine a gigantic, Texas-sized pipeline. That pipeline has lots of surface area, elbows, and welds, and there are many places where it can leak. The bigger the pipeline, the more places it can leak. With the Texas-sized pipeline, you won't be able to plug it yourself. Cracks are going to form all over the place, and you won't be able to reach all of them yourself; in fact, you may not even know they're there until the cracks become fractures and they start to gush. That's what happens to pipelines over time when they're not properly maintained, and what happens to a company's culture as the company grows and the culture isn't properly maintained. It's a natural occurrence with pipes and with people, because neither is perfect. There will be cracks. The bottom line is that bad things happen and culture is going to leak. As you add people to your team, you're increasing the chances of leaks, and perhaps adding to the number of leaks you already have.

A culture leak occurs when someone behaves in a way that contradicts the values of a company. If left unchecked, a tiny crack in your company's culture pipeline can grow into a series of cracks until the whole pipe collapses. Your naturally flowing company culture can't be contained in a busted pipeline, so you have to be proactive about discovering culture leaks and do something about them.

If culture is a way a group behaves as a family without thinking about it—because it's ingrained in the people—then a leak can be caused by any action that's unnatural, that's out of character, and that goes against the grain of your cultural values. For example, a gossipy person at Bryan's company or a person going deep into debt at Dave Ramsey's company, which helps people avoid debt, would be a culture leak because that person's actions would be breaking the fundamental fabric of how those companies function.

How We Maintain Culture

One way we have maintained our culture is by formalizing culture-enhancing activities. We defined a budget and created a cultural calendar. Unless we committed more time and resources to our culture, there was no guarantee it would remain intact.

We also became very intentional about hiring around our cultural values. When I'm interviewing and hiring, I follow the guidelines I was taught a long time ago by a smart mentor. He taught me to hire for the three Cs: character, competency, and chemistry.

First, hire for character. Don't hire people who are crooks or who will behave in harmful ways toward you or your company. Second, hire for competency. Make sure the person can do the job. Third, hire for chemistry. Make sure the person gets along with other people on your team.

I've added a fourth C and have gotten very intentional about applying it. Now when I hire for my company, I also hire for culture.

The order of importance of the four Cs is up to you. My mentor thought character was paramount. Competency is also important, because if a person can't do the job, it doesn't matter if he or she has good chemistry with everybody. However, people do need to get along with their coworkers, and it's easier to teach someone job or technical skills than to teach someone "people skills" or change his or her personality.

Because you obviously don't want people working for you who aren't trustworthy (think of the first question in chapter 2: Is there a basic code of human decency?), you should first take into consideration the character of the person. Character and a natural inclination to follow the Golden Rule are basic to someone's ability to adopt the kind of culture you're probably trying to cultivate in your workplace. Hire people who are trustworthy. Then look for people who are a strong culture fit. Most of the time, competencies can be taught but culture cannot.

There are always some exceptions. If I fly on United Airlines frequently, I trust that, even if the pilot's a jerk, he knows how to land the plane safely. In this case, competency is the most important aspect. It's also important that my accountant be competent so I don't end up in the red. There are a lot of areas where competency matters, or is more important than the other Cs. Yet, in my experience, many companies have gotten too far away from hiring based on who fits the team culturally, because they're too worried about who has the skills. Hiring based on skills alone can cause a lot of friction in your company.

A friend of mine, Cliff Oxford, wrote an article for *The New York Times* a while back called "What Do You Do with the Brilliant Jerk?"[36] The title speaks for itself. Everybody has worked with someone who's absolutely brilliant, or with the salesperson who makes all the numbers, and yet is a total jerk.

Cliff didn't get this far with the article, but I think the answer is, *you don't hire the person.* If someone is competent, but they don't measure up as a person who would follow along the guidelines of healthy cultural values—communication, collaboration, and so on—then it doesn't matter how good they are. Most of the time, especially in this era where the library is called the internet and you can find almost anything within a few seconds, many competencies that used to require professional instruction can now be self-taught.

I was interviewing a guy who had applied for a job in an industry in which he had no direct experience. Even so, his background warranted an interview. As we talked, I asked questions such as, "How do you think you're going to walk in here and run this company that's in an industry you've not seen before? How would you spend your first one hundred days?" His responses were good. He said, "Well, I do my homework. I would make sure I didn't ask the "googleable" question." I thought that was such a great phrase. Most things you need to know can be figured out, but culture can't. I've rarely seen someone who doesn't match the culture suddenly change to fit our values.

So how did we raise our ranking while increasing our head-count? Part of the answer is that we intentionally spent more money and made a greater effort to formalize maintaining and raising the culture in our company. We also intentionally added new people who made sense to our culture, and we turned down some really competent people because they didn't fit. We made our culture a part of everything we do and adopted full culture saturation at our company.

Full Culture Saturation

Once someone is on board, it's not only hiring others for culture that matters—you also have to incorporate culture into employees' work and experiences throughout their life span at the company. In the upcoming chapters, we'll step through the stages of driving culture throughout the employee life cycle, from interviewing to hiring and onboarding, through daily life at work, and even through firing and beyond. There are nine parts of the life cycle, which we'll discuss in more detail in Section III, and you should be aware of where your employees are in it and what activities you should engage them in to allow them to become more entrenched in, and part of, your company culture.

Prevent Culture Leaks

Rather than waiting for your company's culture to spring a leak, you can be proactive about preventing it from happening in the first place, or at least mitigating the damage from an impending leak.

I asked the chief people officer (CPO) at HubSpot, Katie Burke, when she believed was the most important time to infuse culture into a company. Katie told me her company realized it needed to really work on its culture during the time leading up to its initial public offering (IPO).

She said, "In most companies, when you do an IPO, there's a huge turnover because people get their stock and they cash out and they leave the company. We foresaw that and said, 'Let's ratchet up our culture before the IPO, so that we create a place people would never want to leave. Then, when they get their stock, they're still here.'"

This is a trap of high-tech start-ups: They have really talented people who stick around for the IPO, get their stock, cash out, and quit. Then they move to the next start-up, where they work hard until the next IPO—and the next big payday—then they move on to the next start-up. HubSpot saw this coming and wanted to keep people around after the IPO. How could it do that? With a great culture that people wouldn't want to leave.

They foresaw an inevitable disruption and potential culture leak and took action to prevent it. When your company is growing and you get to a new level of compensation and size, people will be tempted to leave, but culture can be one of the main reasons they decide to stay. Rather than saying, "Oh, a leak might be coming," HubSpot ramped up its game and took its culture to a whole new level.

Keeping in line with its goal of being transparent with employees, HubSpot kept them informed during the IPO process. It took other actions to ensure the culture was maintained throughout that period, and now it has regular activities to keep the healthy culture alive. Being proactive about culture on a regular basis makes more sense than scrambling to infuse culture into your company whenever there's a fire alarm—such as an IPO.

HubSpot ramped up its culture game by giving out monthly awards to employees who stepped up for one reason or another. It gives out other awards on an impromptu basis.

During times of high stress, when there are tight deadlines and a lot of work, it chooses to do culture awards, rather than giving out monetary bonuses. It makes its employees cultural heroes. One of the awards is called the JEDI Award. HubSpot makes a big deal out of it. The company's color is orange, so the winner gets an orange light saber with his or her name engraved on it. JEDI stands for Just Effing Do It. The phrase, and the award, reflect the company's culture—*just get it done.*

From *Work Rules!*: "We enjoy a constant paranoia about losing the culture, and a constant, creeping dissatisfaction with the current culture. This is a good sign! This feeling of teetering on the brink of losing our culture causes people to be vigilant about threats to it. I'd be concerned if people stopped worrying."[37]

An Unexpected Secret for Infusing Culture

Here's an interesting tidbit I've learned: Chaos can be culture's friend. Let me explain.

My wife, Adrienne, and I have seven children, and we run our home a bit like a military base. Sometimes when the kids have friends over for sleepovers, those friends often want to grab something from the pantry for a snack. But Adrienne and I respond with, "The kitchen's not open right now." We have a high-level routine. When we come in contact with some of our friends' kids who don't function with routine, they lack a visible level of happiness. By the same token, you can't wind the kids so tight that they experience routine 24/7. That doesn't work either.

Companies are no different. You need a certain day-to-day routine, but when that routine *never* changes, your office culture will suffer. You don't want an office in perpetual, utter chaos—that's not healthy. However, you have to be open to occasional chaos. This is a learned understanding. I didn't go up on a mountain to find it, and it didn't suddenly come to me while I was meditating.

A while back, we had a request from one of the larger churches in the country. It needed us to help find it a children's pastor. Its recruiting system was set up so it performed interviews once every quarter or so. Well, a children's pastor is one of the hardest church searches to perform. If Jesus himself had not said something about loving little children, I wouldn't do children's pastor searches at all. They're just, for a lot of reasons, not fun to do.

The main reason is that there aren't enough children's pastors to go around. They're also expected to do a lot for a very small salary, and they don't make enough money to justify moving their family across the country. The fees we gather on these searches don't even meet the cost of executing the search.

This church was asking us to do the hardest search there was. Knowing how difficult the task would be, we swallowed hard and said, "Yes, we'll do it." Then they said, "Okay, here's the other part: We're going to need our short list of candidates in a week."

Our process usually takes eight to ten weeks, and we had no idea how we could pull this off in a week. On the other hand, we were so honored that a church this size would hire us. We maintained our agreement to find the candidates it needed—we said yes, and chaos ensued.

First, a few of my people and I acknowledged we wouldn't be sleeping for the next week. Then we dropped what we were doing, put our heads in a huddle, and got to work. Within a week, we had the list. From that list, the church found a match for the job, and it ended up being a great hire. That experience became a testimonial on our website and an awesome example of how temporary chaos enriched our culture.

Looking back at that experience, I realize how closely we pulled together and functioned as a framily. All of our cultural values came out during that week and showed us what was possible. Five years later, when we got a call from another large church with a request for another difficult search with an equally ridiculous deadline, I knew we could do it, and the benefits for my team were worth the risk.

The "smart" guy would have turned down the job. That same guy wouldn't have had the experience I'd had a few years earlier, when we were asked to do the impossible, accepted the challenge, and our culture benefited. I thought, *We may not be able to pull off the search, but the temporary chaos will help our culture, so let's do it.* I then told the client, "Hey, we'll do the best we can," and the response was, "That's fine. We trust you."

Again, we huddled together, and the same thing happened. Everyone pitched in, and our culture rose to the top. It was like we were a young start-up again. Our success with that search was due to the creativity of my team. Calling on that creativity was their job. My job was to pull back and allow that creativity to happen, and that's when every one of our values came into play.

It was one of those moments I look for when I define our culture: When we're functioning at our very best, what are we doing that's uncommon to most companies, and that's common to us? Accepting chaos—that's where our team's culture thrives.

The first time I said yes, we were so new and so hungry— and the client was such a big church—that we *had* to give it a try. The second time, five years later, we were a bit more established and fairly well known. Rather than take on the search, do a bad job, and damage our reputation, the smart thing might have been to simply say no. Instead, I remembered how much good that kind of challenge did our team and decided to throw a little chaos their way. I think leaders would do well to think twice before they turn down chaos. It may be exactly what you need to help your culture.

The Secret Within the Secret

It wasn't just the creativity that came out during that chaos. All our cultural values appeared, and we pulled together as a framily to reach our goal. People were responding to each other via texting at midnight. People were making jokes about how many hours we were working. It was all hands on deck, and every one of our values—the way we behave together that we call our culture, those values we have written on the wall—were lived out in a high-octane way.

Sometimes it's the leader's job to accept chaos, but you don't have to wait around for the biggest church to call you or for an impossible project to fall into your lap. A leader can infuse a little chaos into employees' experience to force them to live out the cultural values.

Ed Young, a friend and pastor at Fellowship Church in Dallas, has been known to have his leadership team sit in a circle, where he gives the following instructions: "Everybody move one chair to the left." This activity changes the roles of the people on his team. Another of my friends was the executive pastor at his church one year, the student pastor the next year, and then he went back to being in a senior leadership role the following year, due to Ed's interjecting a little bit of chaos.

You can replicate this activity to challenge your people to take on different roles and accept a little chaos. You can also take on an impossible project or accelerate a deadline. However, the chaos must be temporary—it can't be sustained or you'll burn people out. Be discerning in your decisions to interject chaos and know when to let things rest. People do like routine. They like order. But every now and then, a little disruption helps.

The bottom line is that culture wins. It trumps competency because your strong culture can allow employees to take on a different role or a different type of assignment than they're used to. If employees fit the culture of the organization, they can learn the needed competency, knowing they have the support of their coworkers. They can learn how to do something faster, or better, or learn how to meet a higher standard or deal with a high-maintenance client. You can't push your team in ways that overstress them, but if you've got a good culture, people can handle being asked to do things they've never done before, and they'll figure it out. The culture will sustain them during the daily routine and during times of chaos, and it will sustain them at every stage of their working life cycles.

CULTURE PERMEATES THE EMPLOYEE LIFE CYCLE

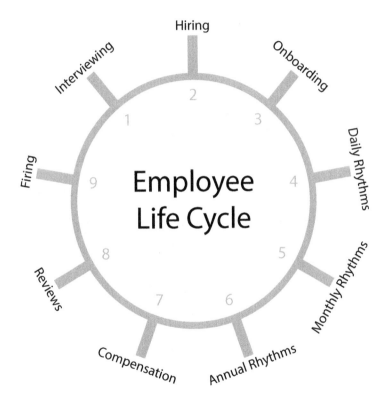

Employee Life Cycle

Hiring
Interviewing
Onboarding
Daily Rhythms
Firing
Monthly Rhythms
Reviews
Annual Rhythms
Compensation

1 2 3 4 5 6 7 8 9

CHAPTER 6

Hire for Culture

E VERY TIME I'VE SEEN an employee who causes a culture problem at a company, I can usually draw a line straight back to a hiring problem.

Cultural misfits don't just happen—the problems are usually present when you're interviewing people. Once you've got your culture figured out and it's in a healthy place—you've realized your particular kind of crazy—and you hire around that, it's doubtful your new employee will become a cultural misfit.

But a valuable lesson I have learned over the years about culture and team chemistry is that chemistry is seasonal.

CULTURE TIP

Chemistry is seasonal.

That is to say, cultural fit is also seasonal. While culture problems are almost always connected to a hiring problem, there can be shifts that cause new wrinkles. Sometimes, when people's lives change, they may no longer fit in your company's culture. They may have fit in when they were single and didn't have relationships outside their work framily, but then they got married and had kids, and their priorities changed. That's a season-of-life change, and it can go both ways. As people get older and their children move on, they may also be looking for a different type of company culture. If your company grows, it will change (and have to evolve), which will impact culture, and some people who used to fit won't anymore. There's no shame in that.

I didn't always know this, but it was part of my learning as a leader. When I was a younger leader, if I hired someone for my staff and that person later left, I thought I'd somehow failed. As long as I was hiring correctly, I thought people would want to stay with me and work at my company their entire lives, no matter what. Now I know that assumption was just stupid and kind of arrogant. While you should always want your people to stay and never look forward to turnover, you have to accept that chemistry is seasonal and cultural fit is seasonal. People change, they have life changes, and sometimes they have to move on. That's okay, as long as you don't have a rabid turnover.

But those exceptions aside, if you hire for culture, most people will fit in for a long time. I've rarely seen someone's hardwired cultural fit change during employment. Winning the culture battle at our company means hiring for cultural fit.

I remember when I realized people *wanted* to work with us. It was when I hired our fourth person, Bob Sutton, who's still working at our company and now sits on our lead team. Unlike with previous hires, I didn't find myself trying to talk Bob into coming to join us. He genuinely wanted to be here, without my having to "sell" the idea of joining our little start-up. When I hired Bob, I knew we'd gotten to a place where our culture was working so well that it was attracting top talent. The challenge for me was to maintain that culture by continuing to hire people who were a good fit.

One of the underpinnings for hiring around culture is to avoid surprises. That means painting an honest picture of the company to prospective employees and giving your current team an honest picture of the person you're considering hiring. This is difficult for people like me. I live in the world of recruiting, and executive search people have the worst time talking potential employees into coming to work for them. We're the worst at painting a picture that doesn't exist, because our job—the whole reason we go to work—is to fill positions. We're the "rush chairmen" of the world, eager to get recruits in the door and telling them whatever we think they want to hear to make them join us. Once we get a new team member on board, we don't know what to tell the person, except we were focused only on hiring. We're the worst at this, and it's not just me; I've heard the same from seasoned executive search consultants, but I've also heard it a lot from founders, CEOs, and team leaders who love their job and company so much that they actually have a skewed vision of what it can really be like to work there.

You can imagine how this approach works in the long term. I'll give you an example of what that new hire probably feels like, and what a company feels like after it has hired someone that way.

When I was growing up, one of my favorite Sunday-school stories came from the Old Testament. It was the story of Jacob, who loved a girl named Rachel. Jacob worked for seven years to get her father to let him marry her. After seven years, Rachel's father agreed to allow Jacob to marry his daughter. However, Rachel's father was a bit of a trickster. On the day of the wedding, he sent Leah instead of Rachel, and Jacob unknowingly married his beloved's less attractive sister.

Jacob thought he married Rachel, but he woke up with Leah. He said, "Oh, no! This isn't what we agreed to!" Rachel and Leah's father's response was, "Well, you can have Rachel if you work another seven years."

That's how interviewing can go if you don't represent your company and your culture honestly to prospective employees. They'll walk down the aisle with you during the interview, thinking they're signing up for one job, and then realize they've accepted a job at a place they don't really like. Soon enough, they'll be asking themselves, "What is this? It's not the company or the job I fell in love with in the interview!"

All the time, I tell pastors I interview for searches: "My job is to make sure you don't walk down the aisle with Rachel and wake up next to Leah."

Hiring around culture demands honesty, and you can't do that as a rush chairman, or by swapping daughters like Rachel's dad did to Jacob. Rather, it means trying to talk people *out* of coming to work for you—being willing to tell them the horror stories. You can tell them, "It's always sunny here, and we have rainbows and unicorns every day," but it won't be long before they discover that someone has played a dirty trick on them. That's a terrible way to treat a new employee, and it's not good for your company.

When I interview new candidates at Vanderbloemen Search Group, I tell them exactly what kind of crazy we are—the good, the bad, and the ugly. We have a great culture, and the people who work here and are a good cultural fit love it. We collaborate, we communicate, and our cause lines up with our product. We follow all the criteria I laid out in chapter 2. We also know our kind of crazy, and we hire around that. I don't wear a tuxedo to interviews or approach them as a courtship, because that's not the person employees are going to see every day when they work for me.

When I'm interviewing, I look to see if we're a good fit for the interviewee and if they're a good fit for us as well. Earlier, I told you about one of the candidates we interviewed for the controller position and how he backed out just when we were about to offer him the job. He had all the right skills on his résumé, but we did a good enough job explaining our kind of crazy to him on the front end that he was able to recognize he wasn't a good fit for our team. While I was a little offended at first, I looked at the situation a little more deeply and talked to the lead team about it. The team said, "You know, he's right. He wasn't the right fit." This turned out to be a good decision, and we've got the right person in that role now.

The most expensive hire you will ever make is hiring the wrong person.

If you don't assess people's ability to fit your culture, it doesn't matter how wonderful their résumés look or how competent they are; sooner or later, they will become cancerous to your team. Then you'll regret the day you hired them. You want candidates to be in a place where they're celebrated, not just tolerated.

Let's go back to the recruiting and hiring process with Bob. I didn't find him on a résumé board; he was recommended to me by one of our best people, someone who really fit our culture. That went a long way with me. Bob has great character, and we looked at his competencies, and even though he hadn't worked in recruiting, we knew he was the right guy for our company. He fit. We had confidence that he could learn everything he needed to learn to satisfy the competencies required to do the job. He learned them and, as of the writing of this book, has been with us for five years and has risen through the ranks. Considering how new our company was and the rate at which people change jobs, five years is a long time. Bob is a great example of how hiring for culture will help you not only attract but also retain top talent. It's the starting point on the roadmap for building an irresistible workplace.

I have a friend who says, "In sales and customer satisfaction, every customer satisfaction issue is ultimately a sales issue." Something was overpromised. Something was said that ultimately wasn't true. When the product came, the person said, "This isn't what I signed up for." The same is true in hiring. Every bad employee fit, at some level, is a hiring misfit. Getting your people—especially the people who are going to be working side by side with a new hire—involved in the hiring process will help you avoid hiring mistakes. I give a lot of hiring power to my team members and empower them to make the *right* hire. They are more concerned with getting someone in whom they can work with. My job, on the other hand, is to tell prospective employees why they might not want to work for us. I'm more concerned with making sure they have all the facts and can make an informed decision as to whether they want to work with *us*. So the interview with me is now upside down from our early days. In the beginning, I would try to persuade people to join us. Now I spend time with candidates explaining what might make them crazy if they're not our kind of crazy.

In my own experiences, and through conversations with CEOs from other companies, I have learned that every time you add a team member, you're adding a variable—a living person who is very complex and unpredictable, and you are risking your culture every time. Hiring people of good character goes without saying, and people won't likely even get a first interview if I have questions about their character. In most cases, competencies are nice to have, but, for many jobs, they can be learned on the job. More than anything, I worry about what the added person will do to the culture.

Hire Slowly

So what does hiring for a cultural fit look like? It starts with pace.

CULTURE TIP

The most common piece of advice I've given people is, "Hire slowly, fire quickly."[38]

One of the top mistakes in staffing—and this is true no matter whether you're a church or business—is that people hire too quickly and fire too slowly. They'll delay hiring new staff until they're backed against a wall, then decide, "We've got to get somebody quick. A friend called and said this person's great, so I'm going to hire them to get that position filled." Or they'll look up people's résumés or profiles on ZipRecruiter or Indeed or some other job board, decide they look good "on paper," and hire them. It's never been easier to look a lot better on paper (or on a computer screen) than you are.

And so I stress—hire slowly, hire around your company culture, and make sure you take more time than necessary to make the decision. Go slowly. Take your time. Don't put off the process when you know you're going to need to bring someone in. And then, hire around culture.

My friend Dave Ramsey has more than six hundred employees. He's the "money guy," the "Don't waste your money; don't go into debt" guy. Having done a good amount of work for him helping him find talent, I can tell you, he goes slowly. I've joked with him and told him it's probably easier for me to place someone at the CIA than it is to place someone at his company. Dave told me the average candidate at Ramsey Solutions goes through fourteen to sixteen interview stages before being hired. Think about the time and the cost of the salaries involved in that many interviews. The hiring costs are astronomical. And this is from the guy who makes his living telling people how to spend wisely. But his company continues to win Best Places to Work awards. It keeps growing. And the staff turnover is very, very low.

I asked him, "Why do you do so many interviews?" His response was, "William, even a donkey can look like a thoroughbred for two interviews."

After you get into the fourth, fifth, and sixth interview, people start to show who they are. On the flip side, you, as a company, also start to show *your* true self *to the interviewee* after more interviews.

Dave's a sales guy and a recruiter. He's naturally going to want to talk a person into coming to join his team. But the truth is, he needs to slow down and take time. He needs to make sure the person he's looking at is the person he's going to get—and he knows that. He wants to hire the right person the first time, every time, so he does a lot of interviews before making a decision.

Do you like to fire people? No one does—at least no normal person. You can avoid firing people by doing a better job of hiring. Take your time and hire slowly.

If you want to read more about firing quickly, jump to chapter 11, where I go into how at my company we use our cultural values to help us have conversations about necessary endings with staff members.

When I'm interviewing, I ask a lot of questions the candidates probably haven't considered. I never start with, "Tell me why I should give you this job." If they know anything about interviewing, they've already prepared a response for that question, but it's not what I need to know, and it's not what they need to ask themselves when they're considering a position at our firm.

Because of the type of business we're in, I ask people why they'd want to work with churches and value-based organizations, instead of taking a job where they can potentially make a lot more money. I remind them that the places we work with are often staffed with volunteers, so they may not be as well managed at the companies we're working for. There's more drama involved. Is this really what they want to do every day? Why? What about this appeals to them, and why would they choose it over a less demanding job where they could make more money?

For our company, finding out if people are going to fit into our culture starts with determining if their values align with our cause. They could be the most competent people in the world, but if they don't line up with our cause, it won't work. Even though we have other people running the interviews these days, I still make a point of introducing myself to every candidate to ask, "Hey, what are you here for?"

Rather than *tell* people why they want the job or tell them why this is such a phenomenal place to work, I want to know what they expect to get out of it, and I also want to let them know why they may not want to work for us. I want to know what's in it for them, not what they can do for us.

The idea is to investigate them a little bit, so instead of getting canned responses such as, "I think I can do a good job; I can make an impact; I can be a valued addition," I might hear, "You know, I believe in what you guys are doing." If people aren't driven by your cause, they're not going to fit the culture.

The Secret I've Learned About Hiring

The following article appeared on Forbes.com[39] and explains why I believe you should aim high when hiring. You can find this article and others like it at forbes.com/sites/williamvanderbloemen.

A new hire can make (or break) your team. Because of this, you can never care too much about who you put on your team. There are countless factors to consider, the most important of which is if a candidate will add to—rather than subtract from—your company.

I'd like to share some of the valuable lessons I'm learning about making the right hire. At Vander-bloemen, we've helped hundreds of clients make the right hire, and as an entrepreneur and small business owner, I've had to make my own hires. I wish I knew when I started some of the things I know now.

Lesson One: Don't Aim Too Low When Hiring

Early on, I was so excited that people would consider working with us that I made the mistake of trying to sell a candidate on the financial package, or the fun we would have building a company together, or even on the great culture we were building.

Those are all key components to hiring. But too often, I forgot the trump card of our business and the key to hiring: our cause.

Our cause gives us an unfair advantage when hiring, because the "why" of what we are doing compels our team more than the "what" we are doing. We help values-based organizations move further and faster by helping them find great staff. And we believe that makes the world a better place. That's a big vision. It's a "why" behind the "what" of our executive search work, and I'm learning more than ever that it's something I should lean into when hiring.

Simon Sinek's TED Talk on "the why behind the what" has been viewed over 30 million times now. His understanding of this key principle is why he's so good at understanding millennials. By many accounts, this generation is now the largest in the workforce. And their market share of the workforce is only going to rise as Baby Boomers continue to move into retirement.

Understanding how to motivate, inspire, and hire this amazing generation will be paramount in the coming years (I believe it already is). Over 70% of my team is in this group, and I've come to believe that the number one motivator for millennials is cause.

"Why are we doing what we are doing?" That's the question they're asking.

Recently, we had the chance to offer a position to a young woman who has interned and done contract work for us for several years during college. She's way more gifted than her years and has a lot of options in front of her, but she's decided to ask her fiancé to move so she can take the position with us. In debriefing the hiring conversation with her manager, her manager did a great job with all of the mechanics, and made a compelling case. But the trump card of the conversation wasn't the benefits or pay. It was casting a vision for our cause. Cause trumps everything for us.

I have a pastor friend who has done an amazing job building a church that has changed his city for good. He's raised a lot of money for initiatives that have helped the community. He is a preacher's kid, and says one of the best lessons his dad taught him was on preaching about giving. He says, "Dad told me, 'Son, you know the number one mistake preachers make when talking about money? They aim for the wallet. That's aiming too low. Aim for the heart. You win that, and the wallet will follow.'"

I'd say I'm learning the same lesson about hiring. I used to aim too low. I talked about the wallet, or the fun, or even the culture. Those are needed components in hiring, but the real bullseye is higher. I'm now aiming for the heart. I'm casting a vision for how coming on our team could be a part of changing the world. And I've yet to see it fail.

Aim higher when hiring. You won't regret it.

For my own company, I think it's a mistake for me to play a big part in the interview process if the candidate is someone I won't have a lot of direct contact with once hired. I'll spend all the time in the world interviewing a candidate I'm going to spend all the time in the world with, but if that person's daily

interaction will be mainly with other teams or people, the interview should be handled mainly by those team members.

Unless it's for my lead team, where I'm still heavily involved in hiring decisions, I give the final decision-making power to the team that's going to be adding an individual. Team members hire their own people. My role is more as the protector or guardian of our culture.

Most of my efforts are spent trying to talk people *out* of working here. I tell them, "Hey, look. My function here is to talk you out of being here. We are crazy people. This is not a normal place to work. I don't want you to move your family across the country and all of a sudden wake up and say, 'I'm working in an insane asylum. These people are nuts.'"

I tell the story of Rachel and Leah to nearly every candidate we interview for our team, and in nearly every interview now, I eventually say, "My job is to make sure you don't walk down the aisle with Rachel and wake up next to Leah." Now, as we interview a lot of pastors, they all get it and think it's funny—but it's true.

I tell them about our cultural values because they have to know what they are and think about whether they're going to be a good fit. We talk about qualities they will have to embrace to be successful here, such as agility and a willingness to stretch into new opportunities. I let them know, if they like set hours and prefer a routine workplace, they need to leave—turn around and go home. But if they like agility, then we can talk about broadband love.

If they have one particular part of faith they think is absolutely right, and everybody else is wrong, they're not going to like working with us, because our culture will make them uncomfortable. That's because we serve a very broad range of churches with varying opinions on doctrinal issues. We would rather err on the side of serving too many churches, rather than too few. And we've named that value #BroadbandLove. Some really great folks who have a more precise view of their theology would go crazy if they had to serve some of our clients. So it's better to explain that on the front end and make sure they don't get here, become frustrated, and create cultural toxicity.

If we are interviewing people who like shutting their phone off, they won't like us because we want ridiculous responsiveness. That means never being fully shut off from work and having the discernment to know when an after-hours email/text/call is one that needs to be taken. If you're okay with turning in work that's only 80 percent complete, like at many companies that just want it done fast, you're not a good fit for us. We want work to be full of wow-making excellence. In interviews we run through all nine culture values, nine great reasons to catch an early flight home or "Let me help you turn and run."

We also interview for culture when we aren't in an official interview.

About ten years ago, when I first thought about working in the search business, I interviewed with Korn Ferry, the largest search firm in the world. I was speaking with the head of energy practice there, Bruce, and he was telling me I was going to be great in this new role—a new role in an industry in which I had no experience whatsoever.

I asked him, "How do you know I'm going to be great at this?"

He said, "Let me ask you a question. You're on a father-daughter ski trip and you're on the ski lift having a great conversation with your daughter, and your phone rings. Do you answer it?"

I said, "Well, it depends on who it is."

"Like I said," he continued, "you're going to do great, because (a) you had your phone, (b) you had it on, and (c) you have enough sense to see if the call's worth taking or not."

That's the same mentality we've built into our company. It's who we are, and we incorporate that part of our culture into the interview process.

For example, when we're vetting new candidates, there's a significant chance they'll get a text message from someone on our team—and not necessarily the person who interviewed them, but someone they talked to here at some point. They'll likely get the text at a late-night hour, maybe around 10:30 p.m. The message will probably be some kind of weird question such as, "Okay, the Astros have won over fifty games before the All-Star break. How many teams that do that also win the World Series? Do you know?"

If they don't answer, it doesn't mean they'll lose the job. But if they answer within the first minute, saying, "Ha, ha, I love the Astros, too," then they'll get a big-time bonus point (for loving the Astros) and another point for answering within one minute, which aligns with the idea of ridiculous responsiveness. If they answer with something like, "Well, I looked it up and only three teams have done that. The Rangers did it twice and the Astros once. The Astros blew the World Series, and the Rangers won it both times," then I know (a) they're ridiculously responsive,

(b) they've made me go "Wow!" (c) they've shown solution-side living, and (d) they've shown a contagious sense of fun, because they're snarky about the Astros, which is fine by us!

It sounds simple, responding to a late-night text, but it's very telling for our recruiters. I have, however, ruined this part of the test now because I've told the story: It's been in a magazine, and it's in this book.

We don't tell people these little tests are part of the interview. If they pass the test, we tell them, "Look, we have communication guidelines during off hours. It's not free-for-all texting 24/7, but if you get an email, answer us the next time you're on your computer, within 24 hours. If you get a text after hours, answer it right away. If you get a call, pick it up. If that's going to make you crazy, then we want to test for that right away."

For your own company, figure out ways you can take some of your cultural values and actively incorporate them outside of the formal interview.

Another method we use for interviewing is including someone outside the normal circle of interviewers into the process. For example, if a candidate is interviewing for a job working in our marketing department, we might have someone on the research team be in on the interview because that person is a fantastic example of someone living out our cultural values. We may also decide to have someone on our team who would be working *for* that candidate conduct part of the interview.

When I was a younger CEO, and when I was a senior pastor, I used to think the idea of 360 interviewing where you have multiple team members of varying departments and superiority interview the candidate was stupid. I thought, *A leader knows who belongs on the team. Don't let the inmates run the prison—don't have someone beneath that position interviewing a potential supervisor.* Now that I'm older and have seen how 360 interviewing can benefit the team and the culture, we use it all the time. The process is more expensive than traditional interviewing techniques, because it requires paid employees to spend their work hours interviewing people, but remember: There's nothing more expensive than making the wrong hire.

When we interviewed Tim Stevens, who was going to move his family across the country so he could work for our firm, we brought in an intern to help interview him. Tim has a crazy amount of experience and is one of the most respected church leaders I know. It was a huge win for us to even have Tim consider joining our team. So it gave me pause to think that we were going to let a twenty-year-old have a say in whether to hire him, but it was the right thing to do. That way, we not only tested for culture, but we also tested Tim's ability to work in a flat organization, which is also part of our culture.

I thought we were crazy for incorporating this method until I talked to Jill Donovan at Rustic Cuff, a bracelet company, who said her company has a hiring committee made up of several people who best embody the culture. They act as a "culture committee" and perform one of many interviews that candidates go through at Rustic Cuff. Jill told me, "You know, you can pass all the competency pieces in the world, but if you don't pass the culture committee, then you're not going to make it."

From CEO after CEO I've talked with about culture, probably the most prominent theme I've heard is that hiring around culture makes all the difference.

Nancy Lyons at digital agency Clockwork is another CEO who talked about driving home values during the interview process. She said if candidates approach the talk of values with the same care, consideration, and sense of innovation as they approach their areas of focus—sales, marketing, finance, or whatever—then they pass that portion of the interview test.

Another CEO who talked with me about hiring for culture, Stephan Goss at Zeeto, a data company, said, "We call ours the 'beer test.' Would I want to go have a beer with them after work? If not, we're probably not going to hire that person."

One of our clients, a large-scale church doing great work, brings in candidates for mass on-site hiring. The process is very fast-paced. It's a slow process of hiring, but it's very fast-paced when you're in the middle of it. The candidates attend services at night, and during the day, they take personality and aptitude tests and go through speed interviews. With all that going on, the only interaction they have with the senior leader of the organization is a handshake and three or four minutes.

I wondered why this church does it that way and asked, "Is it because he [the CEO] doesn't have time for this?" The answer was, "No, no, no. We have to make him do it this way. If he could have it his way, he'd love to spend the whole weekend with everyone here. The truth is, if they get a job here, they aren't going to see him much. We don't want to promise something that won't be delivered. We don't want to create an expectation. Yes, our interview process is brutal, but it's hard work here. We're very fast-paced, and we want the interview process to mirror what you're going to experience if you come here." Putting that kind of trust in your people is a reflection of the trust you have in them, and you actively remind them of that level of trust by allowing them to make those decisions.

A question I get asked fairly often is, "What if a company's in a technical space and they have to hire someone with specialized skills, but that person isn't a cultural fit?" I will tell you, if my focus weren't values- or faith-based but on making a ton of money instead, I would have started a search group for IT positions, coders, and CIOs, instead of pastors. There are just enough people with those specialties to go around while the internet explodes. If you're in this kind of search group, you're already facing an uphill battle, because there's a supply-and-demand issue. I hear comments such as, "Okay, I found a great coder, but he doesn't fit in. Can I give him a dark room upstairs and let him play Halo in his spare time? That way, I don't have to worry about him fitting in."

While you can choose this option, before you hire someone who doesn't fit the culture of your team, you may want to ask yourself a few questions: How much do you really need that skill set? What would you do if you couldn't find someone with that skill set? Is there a way to outsource that option? It may be that you don't need to bring someone in.

The truth is, if the person you're trying to hire doesn't work well with your people, he or she won't work well as a member of the team. There will be times when you will have to give a little on culture to gain a competency that's essential. In today's "gig" economy, there are a lot of outsourcing options that weren't always available. If leaders think a little more creatively, saying, "Protect the culture first. Find a creative solution around it," then they'll protect the team and the culture. Knowingly bringing someone in-house who you know isn't going to work well with your team won't just cause a culture leak; rather, a cultural misfit can become toxic or cancerous to your company.

Entry-Level Versus Experienced Hires

When we first started, I was trying to attract only top talent—people who'd been at big churches and whom everyone would know. While those were terrific hires, these days I'm more excited about a strong intern hire, someone who's interned for us on a voluntary basis and is interested in coming on as a paid employee. One of our cultural values is constant improvement, and if I'm going to preach it, I have to give my people opportunities to improve their skills and their situations. I know that if we onboard new hires correctly with our cultural values, and they exhibit positive learning trajectories, they will move up in the organization.

When hiring for culture, I give extra consideration to entry-level hires. We're not a number-one firm, but we're not far from it, so we have high expectations for our people. In our group, you're either going to improve or drop off, so how an intern or a low-level new hire performs tells me a lot about that person's ability to perform long-term, as a rising star in our company.

This realization changed the way I think about hiring. It's rare for us to bring someone in at the top level anymore, and I lean more toward bringing people up through the organization. This method also insulates our group from a variety of risks. I feel good about the entry-level hires, because we're able to test for culture and I know competencies can be learned. I believe they'll blossom into something more and function well because that cultural fit we hired them for isn't going to change and, in fact, will grow as they become more ingrained in the company. We promote from within when we can.

Our clients often tell us, "We do a lot of hiring from within, so we don't need to hire you to find another candidate." My response to that train of thought is, "I'm all for hiring from within. I get it. People know your culture; they fit your brand and they know your story. But I've got to tell you, there's a balance. You can't *just* hire from within."

I grew up in western North Carolina near where they filmed an old movie called *Deliverance*. I can tell you, if you've seen that movie, you know constant inbreeding doesn't work out. The idea is to look within your business for potential but to also acquire talent from the outside to bring in fresh ideas and create a strong balance. When we hire from outside, we double test for culture to ensure we're bringing in people who are already a solid fit.

Is Culture Teachable?

Ben Kirshner, CEO of Elite SEM, a digital marketing agency, said, "I believe any skill can be taught, but I can't teach you how not to be a jerk."

I don't believe culture can be taught—if it can, I haven't learned how yet. I've learned how to spot what fits.

In the NFL combine, when coaches, managers, and others scout players to go into the NFL draft, one of the common quotes is, "You just can't coach speed."[40] They make all the guys run the forty-yard dash, because you can't make people faster.

There is a lot you *can* teach, but you can't coach speed. It's the same with values—you can't coach culture.

However, you don't want to hire only people who are just like you or who think the same way you do. Earlier, we talked about HubSpot's realizing it needed to start hiring more for diversity. A quote by Ron Friedman from *The Best Place to Work* sums it up: "While similarity among coworkers can foster smoother interactions and better working relationships, there's a point at which too much similarity can actually stifle certain elements of performance. The reasons are several. *For one, similarity fosters complacency.*"[41] (Emphasis added.)

If everyone in a company acts or thinks the same, the situation fosters complacency. It causes overconfidence and stifles creativity. People can have different personality types, and your company should have different demographics and age ranges. People can have different skill sets. But everyone needs to operate from the same cultural values if you're going to work as a team.

CEOs or recruiters are notorious for thinking, *I can teach them that. I can equip them with those.* In all the studies I've done on culture leading up to this book, I've yet to see someone claim they know how to teach someone culture.

Some people will try to fake the culture—and we'll talk more about this concept in the coming chapters—but my experience has been, people can't fake culture for more than two weeks. If you think people can fake behavior longer than two weeks, go to the gym the first week in January, and then go the third week. It's packed the first two weeks, but many of those people disappear by the third week.

When you're hiring locally, you can test for competency, culture, and anything else by hiring people on a contract basis. I've used this method occasionally, hiring my own staff. There have been times during the interview process when we know right away that a candidate is a great cultural fit, but we have other applicants with better résumés in terms of competency, experience, and all the skills you want to see that indicate a great long-term business partnership. However, those candidates may not be as good a cultural fit.

Hiring on a contract basis works well if you have someone who fits your cultural requirements but is lacking the skills to do the job. It also works if people have the competencies but you're not sure if they're going to work well with your team. You can look at it from both sides when you have a chance to try a fit on a contract basis. When we decide to do this, I offer the person a ninety-day contract to work for us as a 1099 employee. I tell them, "In ninety days, you may decide we're crazy or it's crazy for you to work for me. Or we may decide you fit culturally, but you've got to have a little bit more competency." The arrangement usually works out great, and people learn the skills necessary to do their jobs quickly and become competent parts of our team.

Contract hiring doesn't always work out, but if there are people locally you can bring in and hire for contract labor, terminal projects, or arrangements, you can say, "You do this one project for me and I will pay you for the work." Then make sure the work keeps them around for at least two weeks. Again, it's difficult to fake culture for more than those first two weeks, but if you keep them on for a month or longer, it can work out as a great way to interview for culture.

If you hire around culture, you will save your company time and money. If you're willing to show people what kind of crazy you are, and if you intentionally work toward having symmetry between the interview process and the way your work culture functions, then people—including those who are highly talented—will opt out if they don't fit. Allow people to see what they're getting into on day one. Then they won't have to wake up with Leah. They'll say, "This company is the Rachel I married. I'm glad I'm here, and I'm ready to join the team."

CHAPTER 7

Onboard for Culture

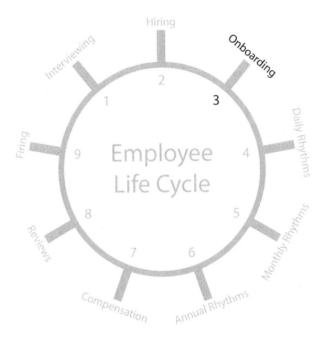

H AVE YOU EVER STARTED a new job and looked forward to that first day at the office, only to quickly find that you don't have any clue what you're actually supposed to be doing? If so, you're not alone. In my experience, that's common. I know it's been true in my life.

I've been excited to land many jobs in my lifetime, then once I started, I sat at my desk for the first week or two, wondering what I was supposed to be doing. Eventually, I figured out how to stay busy and be productive, but around three to six months in, I'd make some sort of mistake or do something unacceptable. Then I'd hear something like, "Oh, that's not how we work around here." How they *did* work had never been communicated to me, so how was I supposed to know? I was never told, "Here's what you're expected to accomplish. This is how we behave here. These are the no-nos." There was simply no guidance.

According to relocation management software company UrbanBound, "Organizations with a standard onboarding process experience 54 percent greater new hire productivity and 50 percent greater new hire retention."[42] At our company, we've built an onboarding system that delivers a massive cultural infusion from the get-go. We begin loading people into our culture even before day one. After the hiring phase, the cultural initiation into our framily isn't over—it's just beginning. The company's cultural values need to be driven through the entire life cycle of an employee, so once that person is in your office, you need to make sure you onboard him or her in a way that matches who you are. The massive infusion of our company's culture begins on the day a person is offered a job.

More than ever, I believe that when a company focuses on infusing culture into the onboarding process, the quicker and more effective the process will be. And that means happier employees. It also means more cost-efficient employees.

Total Life Stewardship and Financial Responsibility

So when do we start onboarding for culture? Before our new employees even get to day one at the office. That process was born out of my learning things the hard way.

One of our values is total life stewardship. I mentioned earlier that the first year we were successful, my lifestyle brought on significant weight gain and a lot of sleep loss. I knew right then I had to take care of myself. I also realized we were in a start-up that was growing fast, and the growth would change from one year to the next. Our people wouldn't be able to depend on superhigh bonuses. I knew we needed to hire people who were fiscally responsible and take care of themselves from a whole life-stewardship standpoint.

When our new employees receive an employment offer, one of the stipulations is that before they start, they complete a course called Financial Peace University (FPU). The classes walk you through budget management, getting rid of debt, and making sure you're living within your means. I've found that if you hire people who are deep in debt, you'll never be able to pay them enough to get them out of debt, because they will always find another hole of debt to fall into. I've also found that if you have an indebted employee, you've got a distracted employee. With the way this company runs and the pace we run at, I don't ever, ever want our team to appear to our clients or candidates as slick salespeople who are running downhill. That is not our cultural vibe—we're a trusted adviser. We're not in it to make a placement. We're here to give good counsel that causes people to look back and say, "They were such a good guide through the process. They helped us."

We're not a group that wants to be full of people who are deeply in debt and trying to close a deal so we can get to the next one or get the next bonus. Before you ever even start with us, we want to know you're committed to living a balanced life, and that includes financial balance. We continue to offer the FPU course to our group for those who want to take it on a regular basis, and some of our employees have been through the classes a number of times.

We understand that people may have had some problems, and we don't expect perfection. As one of my clients says about background checks, "William, everyone has a past. That's fine, just so it's in the past." We run a credit check, and if there's a persistent inability to get out of debt, then the person goes through FPU and tells me how he or she is planning to pull back out of it. Most important, once employees have gotten the job, but before they start, part of their contractual agreement is that they're going to start living out the value of total life stewardship by taking the FPU course on living in balance financially.

When new hires take the course, they take it at their own expense as a show of their commitment to making those changes. It's not expensive, but it's a way for us to let them know that to work here, they need to be good life stewards and they need to be invested.

The Culture Funnel

The goal for us is to make a new hire feel like part of the framily within one or two weeks. One way we do this is through what we have come to call the culture funnel.

We discovered the culture funnel by accident when we were playing around with new ways to use our sales funnel system, which we have through HubSpot, for cultivating new clients. We began to ask ourselves, "What would happen if every new employee were put through the same nurturing system we put potential clients through?"

Every business has a process for marketing to external, prospective customers (prospects) and current customers. It might be an email automation tool, a customer relationship management (CRM) system, or inbound marketing software used to create and deliver campaigns that turn someone who's interested in reading a website into a customer, and for turning current clients into bigger clients.

Drip campaigns, which slowly "drip" information about a company's services to external customers, can be created with these systems. These campaigns are very effective for engaging new clients and informing them about products and services. If drip campaigns work for engaging external customers, why not repurpose them to engage internal customers—the staff? We decided to do just that, approaching new employees as if they're at the top of the "sales funnel," people who are interested in learning about our culture. We could emulate our customer-facing drip campaign and create an automated campaign that teaches people about the culture of the company.

Every day, employees receive more of our culture through an automated workflow, driven by email. They receive emails from me, from their manager and their direct reports, and from others, as well as YouTube videos on how to do certain activities. We call this daily infusion the culture funnel. Much like a sales funnel, it simultaneously educates and engages people so they feel more informed about, and comfortable with, our company.

For example, the day before new hires start, their team leader writes a short note welcoming them to the framily, and we leave it on their desk. Because we assess everyone's communication style early on, we share that information with new people, too, along with other tidbits to make them feel at home. Inside jokes develop over time at companies, and ours is no different, so we're sure to let them in on some of those jokes through the automatic emails they receive about our culture. Over a two-week onboarding period, employees are engaged with this internal culture funnel campaign. They're trained on the day-to-day tasks of the job, but they're also informed about how the team functions as a framily.

Once we had the system in place and tested it out, I told HubSpot's CEO about how we were using its system not only for managing our sales pipeline but also for onboarding new hires and managing our culture pipeline—our culture funnel; he said HubSpot had never thought to use it for that. Whatever tool you use for your marketing campaigns or customer relationship management, you can easily repurpose it and turn it inward to engage your new employees. You already have it, and you know it works. Why not use it to enhance the onboarding process, and get your new people started off right, as trusted members of your framily?

Automating this process and making it part of onboarding ensures new people are getting consistent information from more than one source in your company—the HR person—and it also allows them to interact with people around the company early, so they feel welcome. Every new employee has consistent, tangible experiences with these communications but with a human touch. Everyone else is reminded, "Hey, we have a new team member. Take five minutes to say hello and work with this person."

Testing for Culture During Onboarding

One way we do testing for culture during onboarding is through the ninety-day probation hire, which I told you about in the last chapter. This is a fairly normal practice for companies, and it's useful only if the person you're looking at hiring is local. You can't offer a ninety-day contract to people who would have to move themselves and their families across the country to work for you.

CULTURE TIP

As a general rule, the farther people are going to have to move or commute to get to a job, the longer you need to take to hire them.

In Houston, the fourth largest city in the United States (and quickly headed to number three), we have the advantage of being surrounded by about 6.5 million people, and there's a lot of young talent. We frequently hire locally and often on ninety-day contracts at first. That's an unfair advantage you might not have, but whatever your circumstances, I'd urge you to look locally first. Local people at least understand the local culture, which is a part of your company culture.

Our new hires are told, "This is a ninety-day deal. You may decide we're crazy, and you don't need to feel the least bit of shame in saying that. In fact, if you don't make it ninety days and you excuse yourself, don't worry about putting us on your résumé. Count it as having gone out on a few dates with us and it didn't work out. That's not a problem. By the same token, we're going to be looking at you for those ninety days. It's not about making your sales quota or closing a certain number of searches. It's about, in ninety days, do you fit as part of our framily and can you show a trajectory of learning your competencies? But it doesn't mean you have to learn *all* your competencies."

I made the mistake, as a younger leader, of putting a deadline on learning and telling new hires, "You need to know how to do your job by this day." The older I get, the more it's not about learning the job by a certain date. Rather, it's become, "Show me a positive trajectory early on that's moving forward. If you can show me a positive trajectory on your learning, I'll trust the outcome."

Personality Test

We also like to use personality tests during onboarding through a profile called Insights Discovery. Imagine a combination of the DiSC inventory and the Myers-Briggs Type Indicator on steroids. We're certified for the tests, so other companies can come to us to provide testing for their employees as well.

We don't use the personality tests to make hiring decisions. Some companies might hire only specific personality types. For example, they may want only a person with a Myers-Briggs ENTJ profile, or a DI on the DiSC inventory. Using those distinctions as part of the decision-making process isn't wise and, in some states, may even be illegal. Keep in mind, people are more complex than a test result.

There was a young CEO who prided herself on doing seven-minute interviews. She said, "I'm the queen of the seven-minute interview. I interview for only seven to ten minutes." I used to believe that about myself, too, and thought I was a big dog for being able to figure it out in five minutes. But it's not true. It takes longer. However, the longer I do this, the more I have to pride myself on being able to size someone up fairly quickly. I have to know whether people will fit right away, and I don't rely on personality tests.

Take Tim Stevens, for example, who's on our lead team and has added so much value to our company in the three years he's been here. If I had to decide whether to hire him based on the results of his personality profile, I wouldn't have. It wouldn't have made sense. Yet, in reality, he is such a strong fit. The tests don't always make sense in the real world.

For us, the personality test is not a filter for whether you get into the company; it's a filter for onboarding our new hires and to make sure they know how to fit in culturally. It's a tool that tells us how to communicate with one another. For example, one style of communication some people prefer is "Be brief, be bright, be gone," which is what the Insights Discovery profile calls leading from red energy. This is the case for me, and so that's how our leadership team knows to best communicate with me. However, that doesn't mean I get to put my color-coded communication blocks on my desk and tell people, "You've got sixty seconds, then get out of here."

On the other end of the communication spectrum is my COO, Ben. He thinks more like an engineer and leads from what Insights Discovery calls blue energy, so if I walk into his office to talk about a problem, it might take five minutes or it might take five hours. In fact, we may not actually finish that conversation for a week. I know we'll be done whenever we're done.

Knowing each other's communication style isn't about "How do people deal with *me?*" It's about "How can *I* serve the other person?" We know how best to approach each other to ensure the best outcome.

If you choose to use any test at all for screening employees or for determining personality or communication styles, be sure to check with your state's laws first. If the test is allowed, I suggest making a habit of using it but don't rely on it to make hiring decisions. Rather, use it as a tool to help your people work together better and be more productive.

Get Involved

As a leader, don't underestimate how your knowledge and influence can help shape the culture of your business.

I'm not alone in this way of thinking. At Informz, the CEO—or the COO, Terry Nawrot—meets with new hires on their very first day. After ninety days, they both meet with all the new hires again to talk about culture. The two of them demonstrate that culture has to be lived at the top, so they sit with their new people, maybe have some pizza, and talk about how the new hires can live out their cultural values.

Senior staff members should also be involved with introducing culture to new employees. My friend Craig Groeschel, the founder and pastor of Life Church, recently reminded me (through his podcast), "When you're talking about bringing people on, you need to emphasize that new people need to respect the experience and wisdom of people who've been around." Craig also said, "New people give incredible feedback about what might be changed."

Those who've been around a long time need to get involved with the new people. They need to say, "How are we doing? Should we do this or that differently?" The advantage experienced people have is their wisdom and track record, while new people bring fresh eyes to your organization. For those first six months, they're still learning how to do their job, so it's all still new. They might question why you do the job a certain way, and that's the best time—when it's new to them and they haven't adopted it yet—to be open to any ideas they have for improving your processes.

Share Your History

I have a meeting with new employees in which they can ask me anything about the history of the business, which we call the VanderHistory. Talking about where we started and how far we've come shows them what's possible and how they can become a part of our history. I tell them about our cause, too, because they need to understand why we do what we do—why I started the firm in the first place.

I tell them how I started Vanderbloemen Search Group on a card table with an eight-and-a-half-by-eleven, six-inch-deep portable file holder. That's where I kept my six files. We've always been debt-free and have never taken money from investors. I started the company from scratch, and we're resourceful. Resourcefulness may not be one of our official cultural values, but it's certainly part of our value of "solution-side living," although I'm finding that particular value gets harder to pass on as we grow into nicer office spaces with covered parking. We don't have to step outside to take a phone call like we used to, but there was a time when the sales team had to walk around the block, sometimes with an umbrella, to make business calls.

I still have that original portable file holder, and we used to set it on the desk of all new employees and tell them, "This is where we started." A new hire had to use the original card table as a desk for the first few days of work. "This is how we started. Don't ever forget that," we'd say. There's something about remembering your history that infuses the evolving culture into new employees.

I was listening to a podcast interview with the founders of Warby Parker, called *How I Built This*. It turns out that company has an amazing culture, and some of its culture habits are similar to ours. On every employee's first day of work, we place historical markers on his or her desk as reminders of where the company came from. The Warby Parker people infuse culture from day one by teaching new hires the history of the company.[43]

Right now, we're planning to add a tour of our old offices, which aren't far from our current site, to the onboarding process. We'll use that time to tell stories about where we've been. The lead team will be in charge of that event, and will infuse culture into everybody who's been hired within the last six months. It's an expensive day for us, shutting down our lead team for a day, but it will give everyone who's come on board with us a history lesson on where we came from and how we got to where we are now. They'll hear stories from the heart of the lead team, and we'll take part of the day for Bob Sutton, who leads our Personality Profile Practice. When other organizations hire us to administer the Insights Discovery inventory to their teams, Bob leads the project; he is certified and also manages the assessments for our team. During onboarding for our organization, he teaches the new people about their Insights Discovery profile and how to read it.

As we grow, we'll have to do quarterly tours to accommodate all the new people. We'll incorporate the introduction to the leadership team, so our new people can see how those seven people set our culture. It's our way of showing that culture begins and ends at the top. We want to live it out from the beginning. As I mentioned in chapter 2, culture is identified from the bottom, but it cannot survive if it's not replicated and reinforced from the very top.

Looking back at the history of our company, I have one regret. It was brought to my attention by an employee who had come from a very large church that he helped start. He said that church had taken a lot of pictures and recommended we—especially as a rapidly growing business—should do the same. Growing organizations change office spaces and people, and taking pictures as your company grows helps to memorialize all of that history. We now take turns getting photos at each event, but it didn't always happen in the past, and I wish we had more pictures from those times. I'd encourage any CEO, especially at a new, growing business, to have someone take tons of photos. They capture the culture, and you can display them on your company web pages or on your internal TVs, like we do at my firm. I get more cultural infusion walking down the hallway and seeing photographs of our team on TV taken during an event than I do reading a document listing our core values. Pictures capture our framily in action.

When our new team members have completed the onboarding process, rather than sitting at their desks wondering what they should be doing or tiptoeing around, walking on eggshells, hoping they don't step in something, they've already been asked for feedback, they feel like they know people, and they get the inside jokes. Rather than feeling like it's "us and them," they start to feel like framily. It doesn't end there. We are committed to driving culture into the everyday lives of our employees, which we'll talk about in the next chapter.

CHAPTER 8

Culture Lifestyle

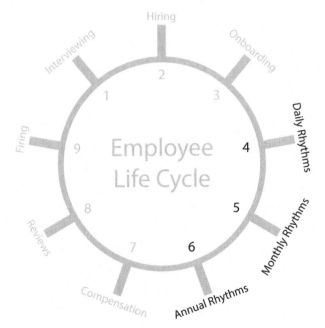

THE DAY I KNEW our culture was being lived out without my having to monitor it was when I passed by the break room and overheard one of our admins talking to a new hire. She said, "That's not what we do around here. Here's how we function in our framily."

That made me think, *Okay, now this has started to self-police.* She wasn't talking about "they" or saying, "The leadership team tells us we have to do this or that." She wasn't seeing our culture as being dictated by "them" but created and monitored by "us."

Bryan Miles of BELAY (which has won top company culture awards) says it this way: "We avoid 'third-person conversations' about culture like the plague. That's when the conversation is about what 'they' are doing around here and what 'they' should be doing." When people in your company stop referring to the organization or its leadership in the first person, as "we," and start referring to it in the third person, as "they," there's a problem. When the culture's really good, people take ownership for the company, for better or for worse, and refer to it as "we": "We have to do this better or that better. These are our problems and our solutions, not their problems and solutions."

When I interviewed CEOs and other leaders about culture, it became apparent that everything we'd done intuitively at our company to develop and reinforce culture had already played out and been proven successful at other companies. For example, Dave Ramsey said he knew culture was working when his people owned it. There was no culture of fear, in which people were afraid of stepping out of line, and it didn't have to be policed by leadership. Culture is working when employees say, "This is how our framily functions."

Our clients feel the same way. They tell us, "We want people who feel like they're part of this house and not just hirelings."

While that wording is more of a spiritualized language, it's the same in business. Wouldn't it be great to have people feel like owners in their jobs and not outsiders? This doesn't mean they can say, "I'm the boss. You'll follow my orders because I'm an owner." Rather, they have ownership of their workspace and the culture instead of being people simply brought in and told what to do.

Some people prefer to show up from eight to five to do their jobs, but that attitude wouldn't work at our company. Our people have a sense of full immersion, instead of feeling and acting like they're here to do a job and go home. Real culture breeds a sense of friends and family, without isolation.

Keeping Culture Going

At my company, we have a required reading list. One of the books on the list is *The New Gold Standard*. Written by the management team of the Ritz-Carlton Hotel Company, the book talks about how culture is transferred throughout the company. Its core values are called the Gold Standards. These standards are written on the back of every employee's credentials, and many companies now put their own values on employees' electronic badges.

Let's walk through some of those core values. At every Ritz-Carlton shift change, every single day—and it doesn't matter whether the shift change is happening in the kitchen with the sous-chef and pastry chef, or it's the beginning of the CEO's or CFO's day—the small teams of people who work directly together have a daily huddle. These are ten-minute, stand-up meetings where they take time to recognize each other as people and say, "Hey, it's Sarah's birthday" or, "It's Ben's work anniversary." Then they have a Gold Standard spotlight. We like this practice so much that we adopted it at Vanderbloemen Search Group.

The formula for these huddles is simple. Say you have five people on your team. Each day, a different person leads the huddle, which means one day each week is your day to lead. On your day, you might say, "Today I saw the Gold Standard of [a particular value] lived out when I saw [a certain person] do the following."

We begin our staff meetings with a core value spotlight. So Brian might say, "I saw the core value of ridiculous responsiveness lived out when Sarah moved this meeting on the fly because we had a lunch with a client come up unexpectedly. We know she's busy, but she moved heaven and earth and did it quickly. Because of that, we're able to have this meeting and meet our Friday deadline. Way to live out the value of ridiculous responsiveness, Sarah."

There's a purpose behind the way this is enacted and the words chosen for the spotlight. The wording elevates the value and not the person, so it's intentional that the praise isn't worded, "I want to celebrate Katie today," but rather, "I want to celebrate the *value* when I saw Katie—who is now a hero of that value—living it out in this tangible way."

The result of this spotlight is that the person who lived out the value feels like a hero for having done something important enough to celebrate at the staff meeting; you have a story that illustrates that core value; and everyone on that team is made aware of the impact of these stories. So people start to notice when core values are lived out around them. Then they have a story to tell on their day to lead the staff meeting or the huddle.

In the core value spotlight portion of our staff meetings, it's common for several other team members to raise their hands and say, "I've got one, too" or, "I want to add something." Those spotlights are a constant reminder of who we are as a company and as a team.

Many people go to work for a company that boasts about all of its wonderful values during onboarding, but after that initial introduction to core values and culture, they're never discussed again. This is like reading one chapter of a book and tucking it away, compared to reading a new chapter every week that advances the story, so you're reminded of what you read and learn new concepts that build on previous ones.

Early Mess-Ups

When I first started lifting up our values, I quickly explained the process with the team but not clearly enough. Our people care about one another and our values, so they responded with comments such as, "Today, I want to celebrate David because he did such a good job with this. We value that excellence around him." Because of how the praise was handled, we were talking about David and making him the centerpiece, while the value itself was subservient.

It can't be about the people. The culture has to supersede all personalities within the company. We identified that mistake and corrected it with a slight change to the wording of the praise, where we name the value first, then show how it's lived out by someone on the team.

With each round of new employees, we would still hear comments such as, "We're happy to celebrate you, Gail…" to which we would respond, "No, don't celebrate the person but the value." That may sound odd, but the culture has to trump everything. Celebrating an individual can lead to jealousy, or to one person's being recognized more than any other team member, which isn't the purpose of the spotlight. We wanted to celebrate not the people but the values they were living out in the workplace.

That may seem like a minor nuance and a picky little detail, but the biggest fault lines start with the smallest cracks. This is true for culture, too. We had to say, "Time out. This is going to sound a little OCD, but instead of saying, 'I want to celebrate Gail,' we want to say, 'Today, I want to lift up the value of wow-making excellence. When I saw Gail do this, it reminded me of what we're committed to. Way to go, Gail. Let's keep living out wow-making excellence.'" Another benefit of celebrating the value rather than the person is that if people leave the team, the spotlight celebration doesn't leave with them, because the values they exhibited remains.

When we look back at the people who have been part of our team over the years and moved on, we don't feel bad or think, *What will we do without that person?* Although nearly all of them were excellent employees, the culture they brought to the company trumped the personalities, and that has stayed and is what I remember.

Culture Versus Personality in the NCAA

Bill Walton was arguably the best basketball player in college ball of his time. He played for UCLA, where John Wooden was, without question, the best NCAA basketball coach ever. They had just won two championships, so they were on top of the world.

According to a 1997 Los Angeles Times article,[44] Walton came to the first day of practice his senior year with his hair too long, which Wooden noticed.

Coach Wooden had a rule that part of the culture of the team was that they were a clean-cut group. On the other hand, Bill Walton was a "Deadhead" who'd been to many Grateful Dead shows. He's a nice guy but a rebel, not a conformist.

Coach Wooden looked at him and told him his hair was too long to practice. Bill argued with him and responded that he'd just gotten it cut recently.

Coach Wooden looked at him and said, "Bill we sure enjoyed having you here at UCLA, but we're going to miss you."

Bill was his star player. The next practice, he showed up with a haircut and clean-shaven face. The teachable moment there is that Coach Wooden was willing to give up his best player if it meant keeping his culture. He would rather keep his values intact than keep his All-Star player. Ultimately, the All-Star player realized, If I'm going to be a part of this team, I have to conform to the culture. That's culture lived out.

Keeping Culture at the Forefront

Every other week, our "culture whip" (a staff member whom I will discuss more in the next chapter) emails an article to everyone about how to improve on a cultural value. The email has a link to a story that tells how one of *our* values is also being implemented with positive results by another organization.

We expect our people to read the articles, and it's not uncommon for people to have discussions about them. Sometimes I hear people discussing them in the break room. The stories help solidify our values. Our culture whip likes to hashtag them with the value they illustrate, so we might get an email that says, "Here's a great article on #wowmakingexcellence." The attached story is a three- to five-minute read and reminds people what we're about, and it inspires them to think creatively about how we can continue to improve our values.

Budget Time for What Matters

We're not a huge company with the luxury of extra time and money, but we do take time during paid work hours to participate in company-wide cultural events. Something as simple as a game of cornhole can play out the value of contagious fun, and one of our favorite events is going to an escape room to work on our value of solution-side living.

If you're not familiar with escape rooms, here's the basic idea: You get locked in a room and your team has to work together using clues that allow you to escape. The game starts with a prompt such as, "You're a spy in Dublin, and someone has gone missing. You have to figure out how to get out of the room before that person is dropped into the river in order to save them." Generally, you're given a clue to the first of a succession of puzzles, and as you solve each one, the solution leads to the next clue and the next puzzle. Eventually, you can unlock the door and escape. The puzzles are tough to figure out, so your team has to work together, which promotes problem solving and teamwork and strengthens the bonds among members.

Escape rooms are one example of a fun, inexpensive way to promote culture. Our teams have participated in the game separately, and they've turned it into a sort of competition to see which team can escape the fastest. They enjoyed the experience and noted how much fun it was to combine their talents to work out the solutions together. The result was using teamwork to solve a puzzle, which is exactly what they do every time they take on a new client or a new search.

My people practiced many values in the escape room, including ridiculous responsiveness by thinking and acting fast, wow-making excellence by improving on each other's scores, solution-side living by strategizing together, and, of course, contagious fun. When you choose an activity for your team, make sure there's an intent behind it that drives home your cultural values. Better yet, ask people for ideas. If you ask your staffers to come up with a cultural event that drives home a particular value, they will appreciate being asked and own the value, because the idea will have come from them—and, most likely, they will come up with a better idea than you could.

Thanks to the ingenuity of our culture whip and others in the company, I haven't planned a single event on our cultural calendar.

As a leader, you might balk at spending this much time on culture and wonder whether anyone is getting any work done. The truth is, when I take time for a cultural event, we get more work accomplished in the time leading up to, and after, the event than we would have if there had been nothing planned that day. In other words, think of the cultural event as rocket fuel for the rest of the day. A two-hour break for fun can inspire people to work even harder the remaining hours of the day.

Employees Who Travel

About a third of our people are on the road at any given time, for one to three days at a time. Establishing mandatory in-office days for all team members can help reinforce opportunities for involvement and team building, and create available dates for cultural events.

To ensure everyone is included in our culture building, we've mandated that everyone has to be in the office on Fridays. We also plan our cultural events for Thursday afternoon or Friday, so those who travel don't miss out while they're away, Monday through Wednesday.

If you have a virtual or traveling team, be intentional about your cultural events so you don't end up with one group—your in-office staff—contributing to the culture and living it and another group of people alienated from it. While you're developing a maintenance plan for your culture, take the different groups into consideration and think through how they can all be part of the framily. Every person in your company is a part of the framily and needs to be reminded of that fact.

Nonwork Time

Google requires managers to spend 15 percent of their time with their people outside of the workplace. Managers are encouraged to take people to lunch and have activities outside the office with their teams.

This is something we've incorporated as well. We regularly tell others in our group, "It's informal, but if anyone can make it, come out for movie night or to a consultant team dinner." We may invite others to grab a bite to eat after work or something along those lines. It's important to make time for the team outside of the office to solidify that bond.

Play Is a Mindset, Not an Activity

In addition to providing everyone with a gym membership, we have a trainer come in once a week to work with our team. This workout time doesn't come at the expense of their lunch hour; instead, it's offered as paid time when people can practice our value of stewardship of life. We want people to live in balance. A bonus is the bonding that happens when people work out as a team, highlighting the stewardship of life together.

I'll never forget the day I learned the term *UberKittens*. Some time back, Uber partnered with the ASPCA to take animals that need to be adopted around for people to play with for a while. Uber clients receive notifications when the UberKittens program is going to be happening nearby, and they can book a time slot for a visit. One day, some people on our team were notified that UberKitten was in our area, and one of them grabbed a slot. I had no idea what UberKittens was, and they explained to me how the program worked. Someone would be coming by with kittens, and anyone who wanted to participate would take a few minutes to play with the kittens. People can adopt the kittens if they like.

We participated in the UberKittens program for a while, and my people had a blast playing with these kittens. They took a lot of pictures, posted them on Instagram, and were smiling the rest of the day. Breaking up the workday made it better and more productive. That's a good example of how infusing fun into your workplace, even in just a small amount of time, can pay off.

My wife, Adrienne, is the CFO of our company. One evening over dinner, on the UberKittens day, Adrienne asked me, "Hey, did you watch your social media today?" Of course I had. Her next question was, "Why were kittens running around the office?" I explained to her, "Yes, they stopped working for a while, but the truth is, they got a lot more done after the animals visited."

It's worth taking the time to have a little fun together. The nonwork fun of having the UberKittens come by didn't cost me one nickel, other than the fifteen minutes the office was shut down, and it brought a little joy to the team.

Virtual Organizations

BELAY, as mentioned previously, specializes in virtual administrative services. The employees provide virtual executive assistance, virtual bookkeeping, virtual copywriting—virtual everything. They get a lot done, and they say they have a good virtual culture.

Our team has had some virtual employees. In fact, we started out entirely virtual, because at first we couldn't afford an office and couldn't afford to have people move to Houston to work for us. But then, as we opened an office and people began moving here, we realized the people who worked virtually were never quite tied into what we were doing in the office. They missed the jokes and weren't part of the events.

If your company is all-virtual, is it possible to build a virtual culture? Yes, particularly when the work you're doing is virtual work. BELAY does all of its work and delivers all of its services virtually. So building a virtual team (and culture) comes naturally for cofounder Bryan Miles and the work he's doing at BELAY. But when the work being done is highly collaborative and involves a lot of in-person interfacing, it's hard to bring virtual people consistently and fully into the culture. I'm not saying it's impossible to have a successful virtual workplace. I am, however, old school, and I think in-person is better than virtual. It's certainly proven true for our work and our team.

If you're going to have a virtual aspect to your company, you'll have to work twice as hard to glue your virtual people to those who work in an in-person space. There's no replacement for face-to-face contact. FaceTime, Skype, and other interfacing tools have made it easy to bring people together, but they aren't replacements. If part of your team is in-person and another part is virtual, you'll have to work hard to drive virtual people into the culture of the organization. That may mean spending extra money to fly them in every so often. While we had a few team members working remotely, we made sure they came into the office once in a while, and we planned cultural events for when they were here.

Our work is highly collaborative. It requires daily puzzle solving. The more collaboration your work requires, the more you need to consider face-to-face, in-office, nonvirtual work.

Leaders should ask themselves, "How much collaboration is required in the type of work we do?" The answer will determine how much virtual workforce the culture can accommodate.

Ben Kirshner at Elite SEM had fifty people who worked at home and one hundred in the office. Ben told me, "I have to work much, much harder to get the virtual people to feel like they're part of what goes on at the office." He spends a significant amount of money to get everyone on a retreat, bringing together the virtual people with the office people to build culture in a face-to-face environment.

What Other Companies Are Doing

One company that's fascinating to me is Chick-fil-A. It is driven by family and Christian values. One of its family convictions is that everyone needs to have one day of rest. For Chick-fil-A, that's Sunday, so all the stores are closed on Sundays. What's funny is that people usually realize how much they're craving Chick-fil-A after church on Sundays.

You'd think having its doors closed one day a week would dramatically stunt the company's growth and allow competitors to win, but Chick-fil-A actually generates more revenue per restaurant than any other fast-food chain in the United States.[45] Some may ask whether that's a coincidence, a spiritual affirmation, or something else. I don't know. Regardless of the effect on business, the company has remained committed to staying closed every Sunday.[46]

That kind of commitment, closing one day a week despite the potential effects on profits (although in the case of this business, it actually appears to have paid off), is significant in regard to defining a company's culture. Stating those values openly has likely attracted people who share those values to Chick-fil-A. In fact, at nearly every church conference I go to, Chick-fil-A is the lunch provider. We joke about it, saying, "It looks like we're having Christian chicken again."

When you show your core values, you tend to attract people with similar values. It's like building a tribe. I'd rather have a thousand crazy-wild followers than a hundred thousand people who sort of think about me every now and then. This is exactly what Chick-fil-A has done by sticking to its values.

Anticulture

Zenefits is an online insurance plan manager and provider that's trying to disrupt the insurance industry. It had a fantastic idea for streamlining what is arguably the most cumbersome sector in the United States, so it shared that idea, and investors agreed. People lined up to provide start-up money. Zenefits hired a great team of high-capacity players and built a beautiful website that attracted a lot of customers. I was one of them.

Once the company got funding, it grew quickly, but its fever for growth and scaling up overshadowed any focus on developing a healthy culture. The situation got crazy. Parties were the norm, not the exception. Employees were acting inappropriately with each other in stairwells, and people were drinking heavily on the job. Even more damaging than bad behavior, the company's team members didn't know how to work together—a symptom and telltale sign of a lack of culture. When we had an insurance question, Zenefits' lovely website directed us to a phone number, and calling the company was an exercise in frustration and futility as we were interminably punted from "provider" to "solution expert" to "help center." Each team within the business didn't know what the other teams were doing—another sure sign of poor culture. The company has since fallen apart, losing two-thirds of its workforce, including the CEO, who was fired.[47]

Zenefits' idea of disrupting the insurance industry was beautiful. However, its execution was horrible, because nothing was gluing it together. In my opinion, a big part—not the whole part but a *big* part—of why the company fell apart was because it paid no attention to culture. It's a classic story of a great idea with lots of funding, a talented team, and a rotten culture. Guess what wins in that equation. Culture wins.

The same can be said for Uber, which executed the most elegant disruption I can think of since the internet began. It has literally changed the way people get around from place to place. I've been using Uber for as long as it has been around, but despite my loyalty, there's been no loyalty program or reward system. Not until very recently has Uber tried to track my usage or get me to sign up for a loyalty program. Knowing the company doesn't value loyal customers, it didn't surprise me when I heard its biggest challenge is attracting and keeping loyal drivers. If you don't value your loyal customers, you probably don't value loyal employees either, so you won't attract those kind of people or encourage that behavior.

In 2017, the founder and CEO of Uber was caught on tape yelling at one of his drivers—basically being disloyal to one of his own people. That anticulture permeates the organization, and the CEO's behavior eventually cost him his job.

Culture issues aside, anticulture is expensive. If you don't value your loyal customers, they eventually will go where they are valued, and the same goes for your loyal employees who are not valued. We all know about the high cost of attracting new customers and employees, versus the much lower cost of hanging on to the ones a company already has.

Our office used to be on the second floor of a two-story building. The first floor was a sort of business incubator. Uber bought half of it when it was getting started in Houston. At that point, there were almost daily fistfights in the parking lot among drivers waiting for their paychecks. A security guard was brought in to manage the parking lot. Uber drivers had no cultural glue, and neither did the company. Formerly one of the company's most loyal customers, I now use Lyft.[48]

Uber teaches us a valuable lesson in the power of culture. It had a culture that didn't honor loyalty, and so the company ended up with employees who were disloyal, customers who were disloyal and, in the end, a board that had to choose to be disloyal to the founder and fire him. Once again, even when it's bad, culture wins.

CHAPTER 9

The Culture Whip

BECAUSE YOU'VE READ THIS far, you're probably thinking, *If culture is such a winner, wouldn't you want to ensure it's implemented properly and well guarded? How do you do that? You talk about a cultural calendar, a cultural budget, and a calendar of cultural events, but who in the world manages these events? Don't we need someone to coordinate all that?*

At my company we've learned that yes, we do. This is another place where we doubled down and said, "Culture matters enough to put a focus here. In fact, it matters enough to put personnel dollars here." Long before I started studying for this book, we decided to have one of our employees take on the role of culture whip and devote 30 to 40 percent of her time to culture. As I interviewed executives for this book, I learned that what we did by hiring someone to oversee our culture is exactly what a whole lot of companies are doing. Our friends at HubSpot have even named their culture person a C-suite executive, chief culture officer.

At our company, the culture whip's job is similar to a political party's whip. The job is to "whip" everyone in line with our culture through events, reading, coordinated onboarding, and a growing list of objectives, all designed around the bet that in the end, culture wins.

Our culture whip focuses her efforts on tasks that specifically drive culture. The articles she emails our team for required reading—which I mentioned earlier—aren't random; they're focused on topics pertaining to the company's specific values that help drive employee ownership of the culture. The same is true for the cultural events. People may think events such as going to an escape room are just for fun, but they're not about the specific event; they're about the *intent*. They're about driving values and culture through the organization. Intention is everything.

The culture whip at our company works on the business development team, which makes sense if you go back to the earlier discussion about using a CRM or drip marketing system to market culture to internal customers—the employees. Just like a political majority or minority whip uses his or her position to "whip" the party into shape, our whip ensures that our company's values and culture involve everyone and permeate everything we do.

Prioritize the Position

If you don't make it someone's job to drive the culture, it won't happen. You can't expect people to volunteer their time on top of all their other job responsibilities, and if you expect people to do it in their free time, you will have a very long wait. People are busy. If you're serious about building and maintaining a strong company culture, I strongly advise you to create a position for it. Once you know your company has a healthy culture and you know your kind of crazy, and you've had a chance to think through how you're going to live out that culture, create a stand-alone position, or at least an intentional aspect of someone's job.

If you're adding it to someone's workload, be sure to shift some of that person's current work to someone else. Provide time and a budget to do it well. Unless you respect and value cultural values enough to make it a part of someone's job, you're not likely to see results.

When we first assigned a person to the role of culture whip, the tasks took about 10 percent of her day. Over time, that grew to 40 percent. How much time required will vary, based on the size of your company and how much time you can have your staff devote to cultural activities.

Allow your culture whip to be creative in ways of driving culture. That freedom will help the person own that role. If you dictate what to do, that brings the culture back to "*They* told me how to live culture" rather than, "This is how *we* work here."

Put someone in the position who already lives the culture and can relate well to others in your company. If you don't, then don't expect anyone to be on board with your culture whip's ideas.

We mentioned the culture whip role to one of the big churches we work with. The church leaders liked the idea and decided to use it. We asked them who on their staff was going to take on the role, or if they would be hiring a new person as their culture whip. They chose to have one of the deacon's wives take on the role as a volunteer.

The deacons are volunteer board members and wonderful people, but having the wife of a volunteer say, "Let's get culture started" doesn't work. You can't stick an event calendar on the wall, fill it with events, and call that culture, and you can't bring in an outsider and expect that person to impart culture to your staff. The values come from your people, the culture develops within your team, and infusing culture throughout the company has to come from within your own workforce. It's also important to have your culture whip situated within the company, because he or she will be more likely to know what's going on and can see what's working and what isn't. You can't outsource culture.

Ownership of the culture has to be organic, from the ground up. That may sound contradictory to what I've said about the need for culture to start at the top, but while culture begins and ends with the top five people in an organization, *driving* culture—and *ownership* of that culture—must happen from within. The more drive you have working from the ground up, the more people are going to act like owners.

The culture whip fosters team communication and community, facilitates the team's getting out of the office together and all the other cultural events mentioned so far. It's that person's responsibility to make sure those things happen.

Choose Someone "Close to the Ground"

When I was a pastor, a friend of mine, a parishioner who was a CFO at a very large company, came to me when he was considering taking a CEO position at another corporation. The new company wasn't quite as big as the one he was already with, but it was a great company. This friend asked, "What do you think I should do?" I said, "Why are you asking me? First, I've never been a CEO [at the time, I had not been], and second, why wouldn't you want to take the job?" His response was, "You know, William, what scares me is the old saying, 'The first day you're the CEO is the last day you hear the truth.'" I'd never heard that saying before that day, but it's probably true.

I'm not under any false pretenses that everyone tells me what's on their mind. I'm sure people gloss over issues when they talk with me—it's human nature. Because of this, having the culture whip close to the ground is essential. That person needs to be close to what's going on. Someone who's in the trenches is going to have a better sense of what works and doesn't work for a culture.

This person also needs to be someone who considers the schedules of every person at the company. When we first asked people to plan culture events, we noticed most of the events were scheduled for 5:00 or 5:30 p.m. on weeknights. People who needed to drive out to the suburbs to be home with their family, and even many who were only a mile away, weren't going to stick around after work. They needed to be home doing homework with the kids or getting dinner ready, or whatever their personal lives required.

We realized the people we'd asked to plan the culture events were young and single, and didn't have kids. It didn't occur to them that different people had different home-life needs. At one point, we had a cultural event scheduled on the evening of the last day of school. Those moms and dads needed to be home with their kids on the first evening of summer break—not out celebrating with their work framily. I don't blame the planner, who obviously didn't know the school calendar. That experience helped us realize that it's not only important to have someone who's close to the ground but someone whose life is also close to the circumstances of most of your employees. The culture events planner needs to think about the salary levels of different employees, too, especially for after-work activities for which people have to hire babysitters. All these considerations can affect how cultural events play out for employees.

Staffing for culture costs money. But the truth is that what we pay for is what we are serious about. So if you say you're serious, budget some dollars and make it someone's job to whip your culture into shape. Without that person, your values will remain on paper in a file, or maybe on a wall, but your culture will leak. It will drift into a different place and that new culture will still end up winning the day with your team, whether or not it's the culture you want.

Having a culture whip isn't just a fun add-on; it's insurance worth buying.

Cultural Evangelists

In addition to our company culture whip, each team has its own culture ambassador, the person who's most passionate about our culture. When the whip has a new idea, she meets with these ambassadors to share her idea and solicit feedback. This cultural "chain of command" makes the job more efficient, but the real strength is in the power of these ambassadors to speak with their own teams and crowdsource feedback and new ideas too. Engaging the ambassadors spread ownership of the formation of cultural values and reinforces the idea of building a foundation of culture from the bottom. As your company grows, it isn't always possible to have meetings that include everyone. However, by using ambassadors, you can engage everyone and build a stronger foundation.

Give Culture a Budget

Cultural events don't have to be expensive, but they usually cost something; therefore, they require a budget. It's the culture whip's job to manage the budget. For our company, the budget isn't huge, but it doesn't have to be. The culture whip has total autonomy to manage the budget and measure spending throughout the year.

In addition to our having company-wide culture-building events and activities, each team in our company is encouraged to enjoy team-specific activities, and the teams have a discretionary budget to support those activities.

Although the combined budgets are small, the payoff is huge. Our people are happy and more productive. Employee retention is also better, which is one of the biggest payoffs I hear about when I talk with other CEOs about the value of culture focus.

When I've asked, "Why do you spend money on culture?" every CEO I've interviewed has said, "It's the best money I've spent. It's got the highest ROI." So I dug a little deeper. "What's the ROI?" To that, they've responded, "One, retention. I don't lose my people. They want to be here. And two, it creates a place where I want to work."

Elite SEM, the digital marketing company Ben Kirshner runs, has been recognized with a number of culture awards. Ben spent close to half a million dollars on culture last year. For a $4 million to $5 million company, that's a significant portion of the budget.

I asked him, "Why in the world would you do that?"

He told me that in his industry, the annual churn rate (how often people leave and have to be replaced) is around 38 percent.

"If I've got two hundred employees and I asked you to do seventy-six searches for me next year, what's that going to cost me? What's it going to cost me in onboarding, and what's it going to cost me in severance for people who leave? It's going to cost me a lot more than I spend on culture.

"My EBITA [earnings before interest, taxes, and amortization] was markedly higher than my competitors'. We all charge the same. We all have the same profit margin, but my earnings were higher because I didn't lose staff and have to replace them.

"When I look at my peers, they have half the margin that I do and they are not doing all of those things; I pay my people more than my peers, and we are making more. It is because of the culture. I retain my people, which is the difference. The industry average turnover is 30 percent; I turn over 1 percent. All of these other people are spending their money on turnover costs, and I am spending our company's money on culture, which reduces the turnover rate and saves us money."

People don't often value services that don't have a cost attached. I talked earlier about requiring people to pay for their

Dave Ramsey FPU course before coming to work for us. If they don't pay for it, they won't value it. When you spend the time to put an item in the budget, it gains a level of respect. Items that don't make it into the budget become throwaway items.

When I started my company, I didn't understand the need for a culture budget, and it seemed like an unnecessary expense. I learned that wasn't true, so now I commit money to it every year. I asked Dave Ramsey, who spends a lot of money on company culture, where he comes up with such a large budget.

He said, "William, if we aren't making any money, there's no money to spend on culture, but we pull culture straight out of the profit sharing that we would share with others, in the belief the money invested in culture will produce even more profits." It's an intentional investment of profits to create more profits.

Dave told me, "Our Christmas party last year set me back over a million dollars." That was for six hundred employees, so if you consider the per capita amount spent on that party, you'll understand it's no small amount. His people look forward to that party. They talk about it all year. It's a big, fun event that goes a long way toward retaining his people.

Use the Budget Wisely

Dave also told me, "Building a great culture is not about building a cool workplace."

A lot of people think a great culture comes as a result of a cool workspace. When we won our first culture award, I was shocked, as mentioned previously, that it didn't go to someplace where you could eat all the Froot Loops you wanted for free and play video games all day. Since then, I've learned that building a great culture that attracts people and makes them want to stay is about much more than a cool workplace. Dave says, "When people want to be at work, they stick around. That's the monetary ROI, but there's also selfish ROI. I've got a lot of friends who started companies and don't want to go to work, because they don't like the culture. I don't want that. I want to *want to* go to my office."

The ROI of putting money into the culture budget isn't to provide a cool workplace; it's to provide an environment in which everyone enjoys working. When you create that, people won't want to leave. You won't have to bribe people to work for you or try to convince them the company will be a great success one day. We've achieved shorter hiring times, better hires, and higher retention rates with our culture. And, selfishly on my part, we've built a place where I like coming to work.

What Not to Spend Your Culture Budget On

When you're working in a Fortune 500 company, or any big company, it's easy to throw money at an event. I can't tell you how many corporate events I've attended that were sponsored by other companies, and I can't help but run the numbers in my head. I look at the size of the room being rented, hear the '80s cover band playing, and scan all the people lined up at the open bar. I look for the intent behind the event, if there is one. Unfortunately, most of the time, the only reason for the event is, "Let's throw a party, and everyone will like working here." That's just not true. The real truth is, people like going on corporate trips because they like the destination, but not because they like the culture. Throwing money at fun events won't create or keep a culture.

Big corporate junkets that have no intentionality or thoughtfulness behind them are a complete waste of money. I'd rather spend money on an event that has intent and drives culture. It's far more effective in the long term than having boondoggles or giveaways. Sending your top salesperson to Hawaii won't improve your culture or make anyone happier about coming to work. Throwing money at people won't make your culture better either.

Amazon has a policy that states, "Our median salary needs to be in the seventy-fifth percentile of competitive pay in the market." When Zappos became part of the Amazon family, it said, "We're only going to do fiftieth percentile pay, and we're going to spend the other 25 percent on building our culture at a place people are crazy about working for. We're going to bank that they'll take less money to have a better workplace." And people have. Now Zappos is known as one of the best places on the planet to work.[49]

The bottom line is that if you're serious about building an irresistible workplace, you have to put someone in charge of making sure it happens, and you have to pay that person. You have to allocate a budget to it. If you put the right person in place, provide the proper resources, and are intentional about your cultural activities, you will not be throwing your money away. You will see a return on your investment, and you'll enjoy going into the office every day a lot more.

Trust me when I tell you that it will be worth it. Your people will stay longer than they would at your competitors, because they'll love where they work. You'll have the advantage of being able to recruit more quickly. Your people will be more productive. When you invest in your culture with money, time, and people, it will make the difference for your company's future.

CHAPTER 10

Tie Compensation to Culture

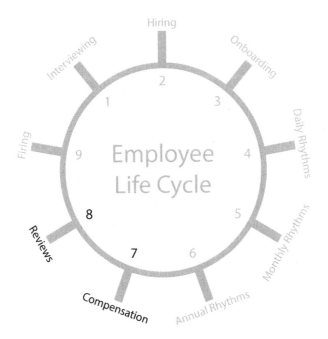

As mentioned previously, Cliff Oxford, an entrepreneur who has written for *Forbes* and *The New York Times*, wrote an article some time back that went viral, mainly because of the title, "What Do You Do with the Brilliant Jerk?" What *do* you do with the person who hits all the sales numbers, has great ideas, always gets great results…and is a total horse's backside? It's an issue nearly every company has to face. The answer is simple: You don't hire the person.

There's a strong temptation to hire the best of the best, the top talent. Remember, though, culture trumps competency. The majority of the time, problems that teams have with specific members could have been prevented if the company had done a better job hiring.

It goes beyond hiring for culture as well. Once you have new hires on your team, you have to make sure they're living out the culture daily. The person who delivers phenomenal results yet drags everyone else on the team down isn't helping the bottom line. On the balance sheet, it may look like, "Wow, that person made a ton of sales," but the reality is that it becomes a straw man argument. If you have someone who's normally a strong producer, but who's being dragged down by another member of the team and closing eighty sales instead of the usual hundred, then there's a serious problem.

If you compensate people based solely on hitting their sales numbers or other goals, you're encouraging bad behavior. In our company, we recognized we could offset this potential issue by making culture a key part of the compensation.

We have company goals, and all employees get a base salary they can live on. As our company grows, our salaries grow, at varying rates. This isn't true for just the sales team but also for every member of the team. Some companies do this in the form of profit sharing, but we refer to it as growth sharing.

Bonuses are based on several factors. One, did the company grow? If it didn't, then there's no money to pay out in bonuses or increased compensation—pay raises. Two, did the company hit its goals? This isn't just about growth but also about growing how we thought we should—was it *healthy* growth? Maybe we grew because we sold three gigantic searches to some random company. While that's great, it's not necessarily the kind of growth we can predict or count on consistently going forward. Three, did an individual's team perform in the best way to meet its goals? And four, did the individual meet his or her goals?

The first three criteria equate to about 10 to 15 percent of the review, while the bulk of the review relates to whether the individual met his or her own goals. We call this the key results areas (KRAs), rather than the traditional key performance indicators (KPIs). We measure results, not indicators, and compare them to the results we expected from each person during the year. So far, this probably sounds a lot like what you're doing at your own company.

Then we review each person's cultural scoreboard. While it's not exactly quantifiable, we ask employees how they lived out each of our values that year. They have an opportunity to fill out a report with that information, and I fill out a report with my opinion of how I think they're doing before we sit down together for their review. Then we go through the reports together.

If a person is living out our company's cultural values, the review goes smoothly. If not, that person may not get the expected bonus. It's quite possible to have someone who underperforms but is living out the culture receive a higher bonus than someone who makes all the numbers but doesn't reflect our values.

The roadmap to creating an irresistible workplace isn't necessarily easy to follow, and you have to be willing to put your money where your mouth is. That means tying compensation to culture. Culture trumps competency, and it trumps performance. Sales will ebb and flow—some seasons will be great, and others not so much. But cultural performance doesn't depend on anything but your own actions in relation to the values of the company. The foundational principle in this approach to annual reviews is to celebrate living out our cultural values, rather than making the celebration about any one individual.

Since the recession in 2008, organizations have taken a more prudent and careful approach to managing their fixed overhead costs. Leaders have been asking themselves, "How do we make sure we don't have a fixed overhead we can't afford at the end of the year?" If there's a prevailing trend I'm seeing, it's lowering base pay and focusing more on merit pay. This is true for a lot of sales-quota businesses, but it's also becoming true in organizations you wouldn't expect. I suspect we'll see more of this approach as we get further into this era of start-up companies.

Building a culture based on performance can force your team members to think they have to hit their numbers *no matter what*. That might cause them to abandon their values and those of the company or undermine their coworkers to get ahead. It can create what they call in Texas a "cowboy culture," in which all employees are in it for themselves to make sure they hit their numbers and get big bonuses to offset the shrinking base pay. Our solution to this potential problem is to tie the merit to how team members function as a family.

A good friend of mine has been the head of growth for four different organizations. Everything he touches grows, as if he has the Midas touch but for growth instead of gold. I thought about hiring him as my executive vice president of sales or as senior vice president of growth, but he wasn't the fit our culture needed. He would have created a cutthroat culture, so I opted against the idea. It's possible I gave up some growth because of that decision, but in the long run, protecting the framily code was more important.

Culture in Review

Culture trumps performance. You can sometimes fake performance, but you can't fake culture, at least not for more than a couple of weeks. Sooner or later—usually sooner—culture is exposed, and it reflects who you really are. It's a direct extension of who you are, and company culture is a direct extension of what the company does.

Ted Baker started a company called QALO that makes silicone wedding bands. They've become fairly popular. He came up with the idea after he got married. Ted wouldn't wear his wedding band to the gym because he didn't want to scratch it, but his wife wanted him to wear it. She was concerned about women at the gym who might think he was available. Ted didn't want his wife to be upset, but he didn't want to ruin his wedding ring, so he devised a silicon ring to wear in its place. This way, women at the gym would realize he was married, and he didn't have to worry about scratching his ring.

In a short time, the concept grew from Ted's garage to a $50 million company with a hundred employees. QALO has contracts with police and fire departments, and Tom Brady wears one when he plays for the New England Patriots.

I asked Ted, "How do you control the quality of your culture when you're hiring people that fast?" He said, "I put our culture in the name of the company." The letters that make up the company name, Q, A, L, and O, stand for "quality," "athletics," "love," and "outdoors."

The company name goes back to the concept that your culture should be a direct extension of what your company does. Ted said, "The company name, QALO, is not some weird word. It's what we stand for. We're all about quality, we're all about athleticism, we're all about love, and we're all about the outdoors. We hire people who are interested in all those things, and if those four things don't interest you, you're not going to fit the culture at QALO."

Ted built the cultural values into the name of the company, which can be traced back to why the company exists. He wanted a quality ring to wear, but he also wanted it to be athletic. At the same time, he wanted his wife to know he loved her, even when he was outdoors and away from her.

When your team's behavior is in line with the cultural values of the company, your clients notice and your company benefits. It all ties together when culture is a direct extension of what the company does.

Measuring Culture

To be honest, measuring culture is an area we're still figuring out. If you plan to compensate people based on culture, you need to have a very clear method for quantifying how well they live up to it. At my firm, we've done this a couple of ways.

First, we have crystal-clear cultural values that have been established and communicated to everyone. If you don't have those in place, you won't have anything solid to measure against. What you end up with is unclear measurements against unclear values. Second, an employee should be able to tell a story that illustrates how he or she lived out the values of the company. An individual's reflection of those values through those stories should be documented and measured throughout the year, and not just before an annual review.

We tell stories regularly about how our values are lived out, and share our VanderHERO (like an employee of the quarter) on our company intranet (the VanderNet) for our teams to read. On that site, employees can find the upcoming cultural calendar and great pictures from a culture that's lived out. Each employee also has an app that houses payroll and paid-time-off details. On that app, people can tag someone, as you would on Facebook, when they see that person living out culture. The tags give employees badges, which they can collect.

At the end of the year, when it comes time for annual reviews, we don't tell an employee, "Your colleagues haven't commented once on your living out our values," and we also don't say, "Wow, you're on the VanderNet too much. There are five thousand badges showing you living out the culture." That's not the purpose of the VanderNet or the app.

However, those two things do give us something to look back on in a measurable form. Managers can use these examples as a way to measure how each team member is living out culture and discuss them during the three reviews we do each year: the April check-in, the September check-in, and at the end of the year, when we're determining bonuses. At those check-ins, managers have the opportunity to say, "If the bonus were to be paid out today, yours would look like this because the company is doing this well, your team is doing this well, and you are doing this well."

If team members have cultural red flags, they'll learn about them at their April check-in, so they have time to change their behavior. They'll hear about any problem areas during those first two checkpoints, whether it's, "You're living on the problem side of the equation, not the solution side. You need to know that's not helpful to you or the company" or, "Your response times have gotten out of hand, and that won't work. You can't ignore calls and shut off your phone. We'll talk again in September and see how you've improved." Then when annual reviews come around in December and bonuses are paid out, no one is caught off guard. We won't hear anyone say, "You're not paying me my bonus because you're cutting corners to keep the money for the company." People are very much aware of what the issues are and the repercussions if they don't improve. We'll talk more about the conversation we have with an employee who has a cultural red flag in the next chapter.

I'm highly allergic to pointless meetings; I think probably everyone is. Every time we have a meeting of any kind, I know I'm paying every attendee to sit in that meeting. The reviews in April and September function very well and are worth the money spent, because they give people a clear picture of their progress. They know what they need to change or accomplish before the next checkpoint or the next bonus.

We also do quarterly meetings to talk about how the company is doing as a whole. Between the two kinds of meetings, all employees know every third of the year and every quarter how we're doing as a company and how they're doing as individuals.

During the reviews, we walk through the nine values and ask each person to score himself or herself on a scale of 1 to 10, and then we compare those responses with my own, and we have a discussion to compare notes. It's kind of like an office version of *The Newlywed Game*, the long-running game show in which husbands and wives answer the same question separately, then come together to show their cards and see whether they gave the same answer. In our reviews, if you thought you scored an 8 and I thought you scored a 7, then great. We're pretty much on the same page. But if you come in feeling like you scored a 9 and I thought you scored a 3, we'll need to talk that through to figure out where we're seeing differences.

Terry Nawrot at Informz uses a template for documenting and measuring culture, and he lists specific times and places where employees have reinforced good culture. That makes the process more standardized and culture more quantifiable.

I'm a strong believer in giving concrete examples. If, during a review, one of my people self-scores as a 9 on one value, but my score and that value for the person is lower, I'll ask for an example and provide the opportunity to tell me why that person thinks he or she is a 9. Remember, I'm the CEO, so I don't see everything. I'll ask for specific examples and ask the person to help me understand the discrepancy. I'm not concerned about a difference of a point or two, but if our scores are four or five points apart, I need to understand why.

In the future, we may incorporate 360s—anonymous surveys completed by each individual's coworkers—into the culture portion of the review, with the question, "How do you think [this person] is living out the nine values?"

There's no clearer review tool than paying people for their excellence. When people get an increase in their paychecks, they understand they're valuable and have done good work. When they get paid less, they understand they haven't met the expectations. Taking the time for periodic reviews lets them know how they're doing in regard to upholding cultural values and why.

I encourage managers, leaders, and CEOs to be intentional about how and when they give reviews. I strongly suggest performing reviews more than once a year to use those reviews as opportunities to help drive culture throughout employees' lives. Drive it right through to their paychecks, which they're bound to pay attention to. While we don't live culture in our company just for the money, we're a cost-driven company. At the end of the day, we all have bills to pay and a family to feed. When you tie culture to the paycheck, people are going to pay attention. That's when culture gets real.

CHAPTER 11

Cultural Endings

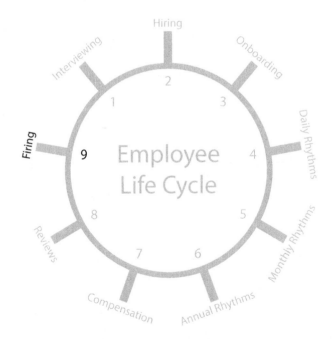

Have you ever had someone on your team who works *just* hard enough to not get fired?

When I'm teaching on culture at conferences across the country, I'll ask that question. No one wants to admit publicly that there's an issue with people like that at his or her company, so then I ask, "Does anyone have a friend with someone on their team who works just hard enough to not get fired?"

I'm talking about a person whose numbers are okay—not so bad that you'd fire him or her over performance—but something else isn't right. The person is not coloring severely outside the lines, but everyone on the team senses something's wrong. Whatever it is, it's not a clearly fireable offense.

Culture can be the litmus test of whether the person who works just hard enough needs to move on or simply needs some correction. When someone on your team is just getting by, but the work is not *so* subpar to warrant firing, the first question to ask yourself is, "How is the person doing on company culture?"

I remember the first time I had to fire someone. He was a treasurer in a church I was serving. He was simply not a nice person and couldn't seem to get along with anyone. One day, when he was in my office, he was telling me a story.

"When I was running the first grocery store I ever ran," he said, "I had this one guy who was doing okay getting his job done, but nobody liked him. Eventually, I realized he was hurting the company because he was dragging everyone down. William, I had to fire him, and I felt like I was about to cry."

Right then, the light went on for me. His words clicked. *It isn't just about getting your job done. How people get along with others is huge in a work community.*

I looked at him and said, "I've got to tell you, right now I feel like I'm about to cry, because I'm going to have to fire you." It felt awful to fire someone, and it still does.

Firing Is Never Easy

I've fired people over the years for financial reasons, for behavioral reasons, for cultural reasons, and even for ethical reasons. In those moments, even though I was mad as hell, I still hated firing them. There's nothing fun about it. The day I start thinking it's fun is the day I'm going to get some professional help.

Ending someone's relationship with your company affects his or her family, future, self-confidence, and much more. Such a decision should be weighed considerably. Sometimes there's a significant problem and the determination to let the person go is easy, but the actual firing process never is. Other times, the person is doing barely enough to get by, and the decision and the process are even more difficult. While firing people is never easy or enjoyable, letting people go because they don't fit into your company's culture isn't usually as difficult or painful, especially if they've already been warned.

This is why my company conducts cultural reviews twice a year leading up to the annual review. Those reviews alert my employees to problems and give them a chance to correct them. Most companies use a personal improvement plan (PIP), or path of corrective discipline plan, to correct bad behaviors. If you don't have something like this, you should. In the church, we'd say, "Let's sit down and have a prayer meeting with them." My teenagers would call it a DTR, or "define the relationship" talk. Once you've implemented a plan, if the employee doesn't make sufficient progress toward improving behavior, you should not waver when it comes to letting him or her go.

Fire Quickly

Hiring too quickly and firing too slowly are the biggest mistakes I've seen at companies. When you recognize someone on the team isn't cutting it, the decision to fire that person can be quick. Unfortunately, the *process* of firing can take some time. There are a lot of great reasons why leaders wait too long to fire a team member, but there are also a lot of reasons that person needs to move on.

I used to think that when I hired people, I was hiring them for their entire life. If they left me any time before they died, I thought I had somehow failed them, or that they had betrayed me. I think a lot of leaders feel that way and a lot of teams feel that way. Why do people have to leave?

The truth is that people come and go. And while you don't ever want a superhigh turnover, which is expensive and a bad sign for your business culturally, sometimes people's lives change. Again, chemistry is seasonal. People may be a great cultural fit when they start, but then their life changes and they're not a good fit anymore.

There was a time I thought I was the only one considering letting someone go, when in fact I was the *last* person to recognize the need to do so. Leaders and managers should think about making changes more quickly because people rarely change, and once you make the decision to let someone go, the process takes time.

Firing Made Easy—Well, Easier

The following excerpt is from an article that appeared on Forbes.com[50] and explains how you can make firing easier. You can find this article and others like it at forbes.com/sites/williamvanderbloemen.

As much as I encourage keeping a team lean and productive, I really, really struggle with letting people go. Maybe it's because I used to be a pastor. Maybe I'm soft. Or maybe I'm just human. Firing people and disrupting lives is no small matter. I've said many times that if I ever find myself enjoying letting people go, I'm going to seek professional help.

So how in the world have I learned to make firing easy? This isn't a comprehensive list, but here are a few tips I'm learning along the way.

1. I haven't. The day this gets easy for me is a sad day.

2. I've learned to leverage our team's cultural values as a way to begin a conversation about transitions. We have named our team values, and we do reviews based on those cultural values. That way, even if someone is hitting

all of their numbers, or getting close to them, we have a way of measuring if they are fitting into the "framily" at Vanderbloemen. Because no matter how productive a person is, if they don't fit our culture, they will drag down the organization.

3. I've learned to make a decision fast but to create a process that takes time. This starts with a conversation to let the employee know they are on thin ice and then to name why. We give our team members some time to make a change. I suggest that you give them longer than two weeks. I believe anyone can fake change for two weeks. If you don't believe me, just go to the gym January 1st to the 14th, and then go back a week later. Resolutions are easy to make and easy to fake for a while—so is correction at work. We then meet (never alone) with the employee periodically to see if improvement is happening. I recommend that these disciplinary periods fall somewhere between 30–90 days, with shorter periods for starker/more serious situations. If the person really turns things around, great. But my experience of true change is rare.

4. Be generous. Whatever you think you need to pay for severance, I'd suggest you double it. The money you spend will pay for itself. If a

terminated employee is treated well, they can become a passive part of your recruiting, telling others how well they were treated on the way out the door. This doesn't negate the need for a solid, written separation agreement, but I've yet to regret overpaying on severance. And smart clients I know actually budget contingency money for severance. Sounds morose, but I've found it's really smart.

Be Clear About the Problem and Your Intentions

Being quick to decide someone on your team needs to go doesn't mean calling the person in and saying, "Get a cardboard box and get out." There needs to be a tangible PIP. Chances are, if that team member's performance is enough to maintain employment, and he or she is not "coloring outside the lines," the problem isn't behavioral or performance-related but cultural.

Whether you have a meeting to introduce a PIP or you have a prayer meeting, be clear about the seriousness of the situation. Let that person know there's an issue, but you believe in giving people a chance to turn it around. You need to let people know what improvements they need to make and give them a deadline to make them. Whatever you highlight and focus on for improvement should be directly related to the problems that landed them in that meeting. Before that meeting happens, ask them to rate themselves on their cultural values. You do the same. My guess is there's a chasm somewhere.

We've had difficult firing situations in which an employee was a good person and well liked, but not in sync with our culture. When that happens, we use a PIP and allow the person every opportunity to change the behaviors, but it doesn't always solve the overall problem. People can sometimes meet the necessary performance levels, but they still aren't a good fit culturally. They might be able to pull it off for a couple of weeks, as mentioned previously, but then they slip right back into the same behaviors. We've seen employees do this over and over again: We meet with them, they improve for two weeks, and then they slip and the cycle repeats itself. This pattern is what helped us see people's ability to fake the culture for two weeks; therefore, we started extending the improvement plan deadline to a full thirty days.

When you set up a personal improvement plan, be crystal clear about your expectations and intentions from the moment you initiate the PIP. It needs to be a severe enough meeting that the employee says, "Man, I need to go home and regroup." If you're not clear, the employee will probably underestimate the consequences and will not make a serious attempt to correct the problematic behavior.

If people don't improve and you have to let them go, be clear about the reason, too: You are protecting the culture of the company.

Include Culture in Employee Reviews

In order to do this properly at my company, we had to include culture in our PIP, and we had to give people enough time to prove to us that they'd changed. We have also learned that we have to give people more time when they are experiencing issues in their personal lives.

It's important to give employees a chance to adjust and recover any portion of the culture they're not living out. Theoretically, you've taken the time needed to hire them slowly so they can fit into the culture comfortably. When people who once fit into the culture begin to act outside their norms, their behavior may be due to a personal issue or change in their financial situation. Once you've called their attention to the fact that they're not fitting in with the company culture anymore, you have to give them a chance to adjust.

I've said before that anyone can fake change for two weeks. So when your team member begins to make changes toward improvement, check in for more than two weeks to make sure the changes are sticking. For our team, by forty days, there should be a steady change in trajectory. That doesn't mean someone has it all together and everything is perfect. If your employee is going through a divorce, that will affect how he or she behaves and lives out the company culture. There may be other reasons to terminate employment, but give that person time, if you can.

We had an employee who lost several close relatives in the span of about four months. I'm sure you can guess that his performance dropped off a bit. However, not once did I want to say, "You've got to go." Those life circumstances come and go, and you have to give people time to bounce back. If someone is past the problem in forty days, dust off your hands and say, "Okay, we're done, and the problems are fixed." But you need to see change in those forty days. In some situations, you may need to have meetings at points throughout the process. Your employee may need sixty or even ninety days to get back on track. During that grace period, there should be a midpoint meeting to say, "How do *you* think you're doing?" That meeting should be beyond the two weeks after the PIP is implemented, so you'll know if the person is faking it or is really making improvements.

Once I've decided someone is done, there's a pretty good chance I won't change my mind unless I see a miracle—a dead man walking. That *can* happen, but if it doesn't—which is more likely—then I fire the person. Once you've made that decision, meet with the employee to let him or her know that even with the PIP in place and attempts to improve, the behavior isn't improving enough to maintain employment.

If you've followed my recommendations from the previous chapter and you're having check-in meetings with your staff two or three times each year, this news couldn't possibly be a shock to anyone. By the time you pull people into a meeting to say, "You're in deep," they should be well aware their workplace situation is suffering, and their job is in jeopardy.

Be extremely clear with any problematic team members, both when checking in during reviews about problems starting to arise and during the PIP meeting. Let them know the improvements you expect, the deadline for making them, and that if those improvements aren't made, they may be out of a job.

Give People a Chance to Correct Their Behavior

Once you've decided people are probably not going to make it with your company, how long should you wait to fire them? If you want to give them an opportunity to correct their behavior, how much time should you give them to do that?

It depends on how serious their infractions are. Sometimes you have to fire people immediately, such as when they're stealing from the company. They need to go that day.

If they're underperforming or just in over their head, you have to allow them some time, and I recommend giving them more than two weeks, but ninety days maximum. Two weeks is not long enough for people to prove to you that they can correct their behavior and maintain it long term, and anything longer than ninety days—say, a one-year path to improvement—is pointless.

There's a reason so many PIPs last thirty days or longer; it takes at least a month to embed a new behavior. Our clients in the church world have plans such as One Month to Live, Forty Days of Purpose, Forty Days of Prayer, and Fifty-Day Spiritual Adventure, and their plans are intentionally that long because they know how long it takes to change a behavior.

Ninety days is the longest I would allow employees to improve, and that would happen only if they needed to learn some complicated new skills. If they're good people but just not cutting it, and you really want to give them a chance, then allowing them ninety days to improve gives them time to do that. If they know in their heart they're not going to make it, then maybe they can use that time to look for another job.

We're a company that values people, but we value culture, too. We even compensate around culture. These meetings around correcting people's behavior aren't about improving the product of their work or about their giving more hours to the company—unless a bad work ethic is part of the review—they're about cultural fit. They're not about rating anyone as a person or determining whether someone is valued as a person. The meetings, reviews, and PIPs—and sometimes firings—are about protecting the company's culture.

Especially when the firing is culture-related, be generous with the severance fee, as mentioned previously. While people are going to walk out feeling bad, when you give them enough money to hold them over until they find something else—and if you're not ugly in the way you fire them—you may find they actually refer people to work for you. One of our former employees acts as a reference for us, even though his employment ended in our firing him. We have prospective employees ask him how we treated him, and he tells them, "They're great. Definitely work for them." Imagine what it would mean for your company if people you fired became references and even recruited for your company.

It's the closing symmetry to the beginning of a life cycle. At the beginning of the recruiting process, I have a thorough conversation with candidates to try to talk them out of working here because they may not fit our kind of crazy. I also let them know, if they're the same kind of crazy, they'll love working with us.

At the other end of the cycle, if the culture's not working for us, we don't tell people that we don't like them or that they're not productive or good at their job. Rather, we let them know, "We're crazy, and you're not functioning within that crazy. We're going to protect our kind of craziness." In that situation, you, as the company, can name yourself the "weirdo" variable in the equation. You're then telling employees they're not the weirdos, they're not strange, and they shouldn't feel personally rejected.

When people get fired, they feel bad. There's no nice way to put it. If you, as a manager, can make it less about them and their performance and more about, "We're the crazy ones here—you're more normal than we are, and we need to protect our crazy," they feel a little less bad.

Firing people isn't fun, but it's essential to protecting your company's values and its culture, and if you do it right, it can be less painful than you think. Companies with a strong focus on creating a healthy culture understand the need to protect it.

Ben Kirshner at Elite SEM built his company to be performance-driven but with strong ties to its values. He said, "If you're not living the values, it's because you've checked out. You're not trying to be your best self." I had the chance to ask him what he'd learned about protecting culture, and his response was, "I've learned to hire slowly and to fire quickly."

I had learned that earlier in my career from my own mentors and experiences, so I wasn't surprised to hear it from Ben too. He said this without prompting or stories from me—completely from his own experiences. So I thought, maybe this is linear. His words confirmed what I've been finding in business and culture as well.

Ben continued, "We've upped the cultural game, and we keep raising the bar. The more we raise the bar of our culture, the more frequently people self-select out when they don't fit in the environment."

We've seen this happen at my firm. Good people have said to us, "I can't do this anymore. It's not you guys; it's me." Later, they'll come by to say hello and visit with everyone. While some companies might have a security guard walk terminated employees to their cars, that's not the case here—with few exceptions.

I had a conversation with Stephan Goss, CEO of Zeeto, about hiring people. He told me his company likes to hire people who are driven and excited to work there, and who can work fast. Zeeto hires great people who like working with other great people, and it has made competitive drive part of its cultural values. People there refer their friends to the company, and sometimes the new hires can't keep up with the high performers, so the company has to fire them. Because Zeeto has named its cultural values—which include being smart and productive, and getting the work done quickly—it's easier for employees to accept being let go, because they understand the decision is based on their inability to live up to the company's values and not due to someone's just not liking them. It's not a personal, but a business, decision.

People change; companies change. There will be times when you have to make those changes. But if you hire well and hire for your culture, the probability of having to fire someone out of the blue will be much lower.

There's a great story about how Zappos spent a year courting a particular executive from another industry. The company spent a lot of time and money wining and dining him, trying to win him over. One day, he finally said yes. Zappos has an intentional culture and an orientation all new employees are required to go through—no matter whether you're an administrative assistant or a C-suite executive. All the new hires sit together and go through the orientation and culture training together. As this one executive went through it, the reviews from the people leading the orientation were, "This guy is reluctant. He's marginally involved." The people who hired him watched him over the next few days and finally called him in—before he'd fully started—and told him, "You have not bought into our culture or our orientation program. We're going to have to let you go."

This guy was going to be a major game changer, someone everyone was so excited about. The general feeling around the company was, "We can't believe we've recruited Michael Jordan to play for us!" The guy was a big deal, but when he didn't buy into the culture, he was fired. Without a commitment to the Zappos culture, there was no point in bringing him in.

The level of employees doesn't matter. The size of the company doesn't matter either. If you're serious about culture, you'll protect it at all costs.

As Henry Cloud writes in his book *Necessary Endings*, "Your business and your life will change when you really, really get it that some people are not going to change, no matter what you do, and that still others have a vested interest in being disruptive."[51] When toxicity strikes, you need to be ready to have the hard conversations of ending things with an employee to protect your culture.

Henry uses the word *toxic*. It sounds like a strong word, but when someone isn't fully part of the DNA of a culture, that person is an intruder to the company. Anything foreign in the human body that attacks cells is called cancer. While I hate to call anyone a cancer, if someone doesn't fit and you're working hard to protect your culture, that person is a cancer. Trying to be nice to people by keeping them around, whether it's because you like them or perhaps because their numbers are so high, will only spread that cancer through the company. It'll kill the culture. That act of "kindness" isn't fair to the company or to the culture. Frankly, it's also not fair to the individual who needs to be let go.

A friend of mine, Sam Chand, is a leadership coach and one of my gurus. Sam frequently tells this facetious story in order to make a point:

> *Imagine you visit a doctor for your annual checkup, you successfully complete all the tests, and your blood work comes back indicating you're healthy. Everything is good. The doctor says, "The only problem we see is we found a spot on your shoulder. The good news is it's a small spot. The bad news is it is cancerous. We want to get it out of there. We have some options. I can see you in nine months to get it out. I'm pretty busy. We can take it out in nine months. Or I had a cancellation and I can take it out right now." Which one are you going to choose?*

Sam said he told the story at a small conference held at a well-known leader's home. When he asked attendees which one they'd choose, the man hosting the event said, "Dr. Chand, do you mind if we take a twenty-minute break?" Everyone agreed, saying, "Yeah, can we take a break?" So they did.

All the attendees left the room and hopped on their phones. I think there may have been a mass firing that day.

It's better to protect the body and get rid of the cancer early than to let it spread. You'll have a real problem if you wait.

I used to wait forever to fire people, and even now, knowing why that's not a good approach for protecting the culture of my business, I still don't always do it soon enough. Maybe you can relate to that and perhaps for the same reasons.

One, I tend to think I can fix anything. I believe if I work with people long enough, I can help them turn things around. I'm sure there are a lot of leaders, managers, and CEOs who think this way. Part of the reason people are leaders is because they're able to fix problems. "Fixing" people, however, is challenging and nearly impossible. People generally don't change, especially when it comes to culture.

Two, I don't want to disrupt the flow of other staff members by letting someone go. Each time I fire someone, the departure creates turbulence and opens the door to speculation and gossip. However, I usually find out later that there's already been plenty of gossip around the person. That brings me to the third reason, which is closely related to this one.

The third reason I sometimes wait too long is because I'm concerned I might be missing something because everyone else seems to feel the person belongs there. Everyone else seems to like the person. Wouldn't people say something to me if there was something out of whack on their team? One of my mentors once told me, "William, by the time the senior leader realizes somebody probably ought to move on, everyone else has already realized it, because the senior leader is usually the last one to figure it out."

Finally, the fourth reason I delay firing people is because I don't want to hurt anyone. Being fired is hard on employees and their families, and I don't want to be that source of pain. While there are some ways to soften the blow, if the person isn't keeping up and doesn't fit with our kind of crazy, then he or she is probably as unhappy as I am with the situation. If it's handled well, initiating the transition may actually help that person after the departure.

Why I Don't Always Fire People as Quickly as I Should

The following excerpt is from an article that appeared on Forbes.com[52] and explains why I sometimes wait to fire a person, even when I know I shouldn't. You can find this article and others like it at forbes.com/sites/williamvanderbloemen.

My softness has made me one of the chief sinners when it comes to the sin of hiring too quickly and firing too slowly. Here are some of the thoughts that go through my head. Can you relate?

1. I tend to think I can fix anything, and if I just work with the person long enough, they'll turn around. That hasn't worked for me. I guess I'm not the savior I thought I was.

2. I don't want to disrupt the boat with other staff by letting someone go and causing team turbulence, gossip, etc. But I've found that most of the time, the gossip has been going on for a while about the very employee I'm trying to protect.

3. I don't want to fire someone everyone else thinks should be on the team. One of my mentors taught me long ago, "William, by the time the senior leader realizes someone probably ought to move on, then he's likely the last person on the team to figure it out." The truth is that the person you've been wondering about is likely someone your whole team has been wondering about. If it's not addressed, sooner or later, your team will begin to question why you haven't dealt with it.

4. I don't want to hurt anyone. Firing is hard on an employee and their family, and I don't want to be the source of that pain. But I've found some ways to soften the blow, and I've realized over the years that if the person isn't keeping up with the rest of the team, they're likely as unhappy as I am with the situation. In the end, if it's handled well, initiating a transition can actually help the person who is leaving.

There's a reason leaders are usually the last to know when it's time for a particular employee to move on, but there's a caveat, because they're not the *absolute* last. As I've said before, your first day in management is the last day you hear the truth. Leaders are generally removed from the trenches, with minor exceptions. They're no longer "in the know" with regard to the day-to-day workings of the team, and their team protects them from knowing everything.

However, the truth is, the last one to know is the person who needs to leave.

The Future Belongs to the Cultured

I STARTED WRITING THIS BOOK with the intention of telling the story of Vanderbloemen Search Group—how my company's culture developed and how I'm still working to protect it. My firm has won awards for culture because my team and I have created an irresistible workplace. I wanted to draw a roadmap for others to follow, so they could create an irresistible workplace, too.

As I began to reverse-engineer our progress, it occurred to me that basing my story solely on my own experience was pretty arrogant. Other companies had won culture awards—why not reach out to them and see what advice they had to offer?

I handed my executive assistant a copy of *Entrepreneur* magazine that listed all the winners. "Go find these CEOs," I said.

She tracked down a lot of CEOs on the list, and I talked with many of them. I discovered that the early adopters of culture are the ones talking about it—over and over and over again—and the talk is spreading quickly. I speak at conferences about strategy, hiring, and firing, but when I start talking about culture, people ask the most questions, and they linger to ask more. Similarly, the articles I write about culture for *Forbes*, *Fortune*, and other publications receive the most traction.

My prediction is that building culture into companies is going to become more and more important in the coming years. As the millennial generation—a generation that's waiting longer to get married and start a family, made up of young people who change jobs more often than their predecessors—continues to enter the workplace, they're looking for more than a job. They're looking for a framily. Leaders who figure out their culture are going to have a hiring advantage and will be able to keep people longer. If you can increase your retention by keeping people on your staff one more year, you'll benefit financially. The cost of *keeping* a good person versus *finding* another good person is very small by comparison.

According to a Gallup study,[53] we're living in a country where two-thirds of Americans hate their jobs. What would happen if, in the future, two-thirds of Americans loved their jobs? What if people talked about their former employers as good people at great companies? What would happen if instead of having to bribe people to work for you, they were lining up outside your door saying, "Can I work for you?" That's when you'll know you're focusing on culture.

When leaders and their teams commit to creating a healthy workplace and focus on culture, they won't see it as something urgent, expensive, or even time-consuming. In the end, they'll see it as an investment that will keep their best people around, and those people will refer other great people.

We have to search for talent. And while there will always be a war for the best talent, the strongest army will be the one that knows its culture. The future doesn't belong to the talented but to the cultured, because culture trumps everything. Culture outlasts the people who come and go. Culture creates an irresistible workplace. If you're reading this and you follow my advice, you may never need to hire me to recruit for your team. I may very well be putting myself out of a job.

At the same time, I've been getting more and more calls from places that aren't churches and aren't any kind of company we've seen before. They'll say, "I have to find someone who fits our culture. We know you've never done a search in this industry, for this position, or these competencies, but we trust you know the culture." Company talent searches are changing, and as they do, we're becoming experts on cultural matching, instead of just finding people with the right job skills.

It's Your Turn

What would it be like if most people in the United States *loved* their jobs? Instead of two-thirds of the country hating their jobs, a future with happy workers would be a future with a winning economy. I hope we get to a time when, whether people stay or leave a job, they refer their friends to that company. That vision is possible, but it begins with you. It begins when you commit to figuring out what kind of crazy your company is and what kind of crazy your people are, and then driving that crazy throughout every part of your organization. If you commit to doing that, then you're making a commitment to a successful future.

Your culture has already happened—likely by accident. And whether you know it or not, it is winning at your workplace. But by reading this book, and learning from my company's journey, you're well on your way toward creating an intentional, winning culture and a workplace that's irresistible.

You're not on your own. There are resources available to help you start your own journey in building an irresistible workplace. Beginning with the roadmap we've discussed in this book, my team at Vanderbloemen Search Group has built a tool that will help you tailor your own approach to define the values that make your company what it is—your own kind of crazy—and help you build and protect a workplace where culture wins. Reach out to us at vanderbloemen.com or (713) 300-9665 to get started

ENDNOTES

Introduction

1 "The 25 Best Small-Company Cultures in 2015," *Entrepreneur*, November 4, 2015, accessed September 18, 2017, https://www.entrepreneur.com/article/252324.

2 Madison Henry, "Best Places to Work: Small Companies," *Houston Business Journal*, October 9, 2015, accessed September 18, 2017, https://www.bizjournals.com/houston/subscriber-only/2015/10/09/2015-best-places-to-work-small.html.

3 Olivia Pulsinelli, "HBJ Reveals the Best Places to Work Rankings for 2016," *Houston Business Journal*, October 12, 2016, accessed September 18, 2017, https://www.bizjournals.com/houston/news/2016/10/12/hbj-reveals-the-best-places-to-work-rankings-for.html#g55.

4 "Small-Sized Companies: The Best Company Cultures in 2017," *Entrepreneur*, February 21, 2017, accessed September 18, 2017, https://www.entrepreneur.com/article/289219.

5 "State of the American Workplace," Gallup News, accessed September 16, 2017, http://www.gallup.com/

reports/199961/state-american-workplace-report-2017.
aspx.

6   Julie Kantor, "High Turnover Costs Way More Than You
    Think," *Huffington Post*, February 11, 2016, accessed
    September 6, 2017, http://www.huffingtonpost.com/
    julie-kantor/high-turnover-costs-way-more-than-you-
    think_b_9197238.html.

Chapter One

7   Simon Sinek, *Start With Why: How Great Leaders Inspire
    Everyone to Take Action* (New York: Penguin, 2009).
8   Laszlo Bock, *Work Rules! Insights From Inside Google
    That Will Transform How You Live and Lead* (New York:
    Hachette, 2015), 32.
9   Geert Hofstede, Gert Jan Hofstede, and Michael Minkov,
    Cultures and Organizations: Software of the Mind, 3rd ed.
    (New York: McGraw-Hill, 2010).
10 "Gallup Analysis: Millennials, Marriage and Family,"
    Gallup News, May 19, 2016, accessed September 16,
    2017, http://news.gallup.com/poll/191462/gallup-analysis-
    millennials-marriage-family.aspx.
11 "The Millennial Generation Is on the Move," rentblog,
    Rent.com, accessed September 16, 2017, https://blog.rent.
    com/the-millennial-generation-on-the-move.
12 John A. Byrne, "Over a Third of Stan-
    ford MBAs Do Startups," Poets & Quants,
    July 10, 2017, accessed September 16, 2017,

https://poetsandquants.com/2017/07/10/
more-than-a-third-of-stanford-mit-mbas-doing-startups.

13 Nathan Allen, "Why MBAs Would Rather Intern at
This Little-Known Startup than at McKinsey," Poets &
Quants, August 12, 2015, accessed September 16, 2017,
https://qz.com/476324/why-mbas-would-rather-intern-at-
this-little-known-startup-than-at-mckinsey.

14 Ray Kurzweil and Chris Meyer, "Understanding the
Accelerating Rate of Change," Kurzweil, May 2, 2003,
accessed September 16, 2017, http://www.kurzweilai.net/
understanding-the-accelerating-rate-of-change.

Chapter Two

15 Brent Spilkin, Reed Hastings, et al., "The Netflix Culture
Document. A Template for Culture in Your Company,"
Netflix via LinkedIn SlideShare, August 19, 2015,
accessed September 16, 2017, https://www.slideshare.net/
brentspilkin/the-netflix-culture-document-a-template-for-
culture-in-your-company.

16 Ken Silverstein, "Enron, Ethics and Today's
Corporate Values," Forbes, May 14, 2013,
accessed September 16, 2017, https://www.
forbes.com/sites/kensilverstein/2013/05/14/
enron-ethics-and-todays-corporate-values/#a074b3a5ab81.

17 Nelson D. Schwartz, "In Hiring, a Friend in
Need Is a Prospect, Indeed," The New York Times,
January 27, 2013, accessed September 6, 2017,
http://www.nytimes.com/2013/01/28/business/

employers-increasingly-rely-on-internal-referrals-in-hiring.
html?mcubz=1.

18 Krystal D'Costa, "Seeing Is Believing: The Story Behind
Henry Heinz's Condiment Empire," *Scientific American*,
March 26, 2012, accessed September 16, 2017, https://
blogs.scientificamerican.com/anthropology-in-practice/
seeing-is-believing-the-story-behind-henry-heinzs-condi-
ment-empire.

19 Steven Overly, "What Uber Drivers Think About
CEO Travis Kalanick Yelling at One of Their
Own," *The Washington Post*, March 1, 2017,
accessed September 16, 2017, https://www.wash-
ingtonpost.com/news/innovations/wp/2017/03/01/
what-uber-drivers-think-about-ceo-travis-kalanick-yelling-
at-one-of-their-own/?utm_term=.6b29471d1585.

20 Benson Smith and Tony Rutigliano, "The Truth About
Turnover," Gallup News, February 4, 2002, accessed
September 16, 2017, http://news.gallup.com/business-
journal/316/truth-about-turnover.aspx.

21 Marshall Goldsmith and Mark Reiter, *What Got You Here
Won't Get You There: How Successful People Become Even
More Successful* (New York: Hyperion, 2007).

22 Amy Adkins, "Millennials: The Job-Hopping Generation,"
Business Journal, May 12, 2016, accessed August 24, 2017,
http://www.gallup.com/businessjournal/191459/millen-
nials-job-hopping-generation.aspx.

23 Liyan Chen, "At $68 Billion Valuation, Uber Will
Be Bigger Than GM, Ford, and Honda," *Forbes*,
December 4, 2015, accessed September 16, 2017,

https://www.forbes.com/sites/liyanchen/2015/12/04/
at-68-billion-valuation-uber-will-be-bigger-than-gm-ford-
and-honda/#6789aee632e3.

24 Mike Isaac, "Uber Founder Travis Kalanick Resigns
as C.E.O.," *The New York Times*, June 21, 2017,
accessed September 16, 2017, https://www.nytimes.
com/2017/06/21/technology/uber-ceo-travis-kalanick.
html?mcubz=1.

25 William Vanderbloemen, "Why United Is Coming
Back, and Why Uber Is Not," *Forbes*, May 17, 2017,
accessed August 1, 2017, https://www.forbes.com/sites/
williamvanderbloemen/2017/05/17/why-united-is-coming-
back-and-why-uber-is-not/#77683b0324ee.

Chapter Three

26 Bock, *Work Rules!*, 40.

27 Chris Getman, "Why Your B2B Lead Response
Time Is Killing Your Business," HubSpot,
November 24, 2014, accessed August 1,
2017, https://blog.hubspot.com/insiders/
why-your-b2b-lead-response-time-is-killing-your-business.

28 "About Us," Connexus Church, accessed August 30, 2017,
http://connexuschurch.com/about-us/#our-team.

29 Dan Lyons, *Disrupted: My Misadventure in the Start-Up
Bubble* (New York: Hachette, 2016).

30 Ilan Mochari, "Yes, Dan Lyons' *Disrupted* Is a Juicy Startup
Memoir. It's Also Something More Poignant," Slate, April
15, 2016, accessed August 1, 2017, http://www.slate.com/

blogs/moneybox/2016/04/15/disrupted_by_dan_lyons_is_
more_than_just_a_take_down_of_startup_hubspot.html.

31 Henry Franco, "HubSpot Named Boston's #1 Best Places
to Work by the *Boston Business Journal*," HubSpot, July 24,
2016, accessed August 28, 2017, https://www.hubspot.
com/company-news/hubspot-named-bostons-1-best-
places-to-work-by-the-boston-business-journal.

32 Reed Hastings, "Seven Aspects of Our Culture," Netflix
via LinkedIn SlideShare, August 1, 2009, accessed
August 1, 2017, https://www.slideshare.net/reed2001/
culture-1798664/4-Seven_Aspects_of_our_Culture.

Chapter Four

33 Bock, *Work Rules!*, 58.

34 Ron Friedman, *The Best Place to Work: The Art and Science
of Creating an Extraordinary Workplace* (New York: Perigee,
2014), 37.

35 Friedman, *The Best Place to Work*, 45.

Chapter Five

36 Cliff Oxford, "What Do You Do With the Brilliant Jerk?"
The New York Times, September 26, 2012, accessed August
1, 2017, https://boss.blogs.nytimes.com/2012/09/26/
what-do-you-do-with-the-brilliant-jerk/?_r=0&mcubz=0.

37 Bock, *Work Rules!*, 52.

Chapter Six

38 William Vanderbloemen, "The Single Biggest Hiring Mistake I've Seen Leaders Make," *Forbes*, June 28, 2017, accessed August 1, 2017, https://www.forbes.com/sites/williamvanderbloemen/2017/06/28/the-single-biggest-hiring-mistake-ive-seen-leaders-make/#622d37ae366f.

39 William Vanderbloemen, "The Secret I've Learned About Hiring," *Forbes*, June 27, 2017, accessed September 15, 2017, https://www.forbes.com/sites/williamvanderbloemen/2017/06/27/thesecretivelearnedabouthiring/#62e3e2684793.

40 Ron Zook, "You Can't Coach Speed," Packers video, 8:45. November 21, 2016, accessed August 1, 2017, http://www.packers.com/media-center/videos/Ron-Zook-You-cant-coach-speed/2964b9ec-9862-4958-be4d-0815dc45d3cf.

41 Friedman, *The Best Place to Work*, 243.

Chapter Seven

42 Aria Solar, "Is Your Onboarding Process Broken?" UrbanBound, January 12, 2015, accessed August 1, 2017, http://www.urbanbound.com/blog/slideshare-is-your-onboarding-process-broken.

43 "Warby Parker: Dave Gilboa and Neil Blumenthal," How I Built This With Guy Raz, NPR, podcast audio, December 25, 2016, accessed August 1, 2017, http://one.npr.org/?sharedMediaId=506455305:506610651.

Chapter Eight

44 Tim Kawakami, "Players Broke Rules, but They Didn't Break Wooden's Bruins," *Los Angeles Times*, October 11, 1997, accessed September 27, 2017, http://articles.latimes.com/1997/oct/11/sports/sp-41682.

45 Hayley Peterson, "Why Chick-fil-A's Restaurants Sell 4 Times As Much As KFC's," *Business Insider*, August 1, 2017, accessed September 28, 2017, http://www.businessinsider.com/why-chick-fil-a-is-so-successful-2017-8.

46 Nathan Rousseau Smith, "Debunked: Chick-fil-A Is Closed on Sundays for Religious Reasons," Finance, AOL, February 27, 2017, accessed September 16, 2017, https://www.aol.com/article/finance/2017/02/27/debunked-chick-fil-a-is-closed-on-sundays-for-religious-reasons/21722935.

47 Farhad Manjoo, "Zenefits Scandal Highlights Perils of Hypergrowth at Start-Ups," *The New York Times*, February 17, 2016, accessed August 1, 2017, http://one.npr.org/?sharedMediaId=506455305:506610651.

48 William Vanderbloemen, "How Uber's CEO Missed the Moment That Could Save His Company," *Forbes*, May 2, 2017, accessed August 1, 2017, https://www.forbes.com/sites/williamvanderbloemen/2017/05/02/uber-ceo-misses-moment/#797fd85f656e.

Chapter Nine

49 Joseph A. Michelli, *The Zappos Experience: 5 Principles to Inspire, Engage, and WOW* (New York: McGraw-Hill, 2012), 71.

Chapter Eleven

50 William Vanderbloemen, "Firing Made Easy. Well, Easier," *Forbes*, June 29, 2017, accessed August 1, 2017, https://www.forbes.com/sites/williamvanderbloemen/2017/06/29/firingmadeeasywelleasiier/#c00244148228.

51 Henry Cloud, *Necessary Endings: The Employees, Businesses, and Relationships That All of Us Have to Give Up in Order to Move Forward* (New York: Harper-Collins, 2010), 48.

52 William Vanderbloemen, "Firing Made Easy. Well, Easier," *Forbes*, June 29, 2017, accessed August 1, 2017, https://www.forbes.com/sites/williamvanderbloemen/2017/06/29/firingmadeeasywelleasiier/#c00244148228.

Conclusion

53 Anna Robaton, "Why So Many Americans Hate Their Jobs," Moneywatch, CBS News, March 31, 2017, accessed September 16, 2017, https://www.cbsnews.com/news/why-so-many-americans-hate-their-jobs/.

ABOUT THE AUTHOR

William Vanderbloemen is an entrepreneur, pastor, speaker, author, and CEO and founder of Vanderbloemen Search Group, an executive search firm serving churches, ministries, and faith-based organizations. He is a regular contributor to several major publications including *Fortune*, *Outreach* magazine, and *Forbes*, where he covers topics about having a strong faith and building a business. He has also been published through *Fast Company*, *Entrepreneur*, and *Inc.*

Under his leadership, Vanderbloemen Search Group has won several culture awards and was named #24 on Forbes' Best Executive Recruiting Firms in America. In 2015 and 2016, Vanderbloemen Search Group placed in the top 5 of Entrepreneur.com's Top Company Culture – Small Business Category in the nation and top 6 of Houston's Best Places to Work by *Houston Business Journal*.

Culture Wins is William's third book following *NEXT: Pastoral Succession That Works* (2014) and *SEARCH: The Pastoral Search Committee Handbook* (2016). William holds degrees from Wake Forest University and Princeton Theological Seminary.

William, his wife Adrienne, their seven children, and poodle Moses live in Houston, Texas. In his free time, William enjoys running, working out, and caddying for his kids, who are now better golfers than he is.

the
culture
tool

HOW HEALTHY IS YOUR TEAM?

- - - - - -

The Culture Tool
is a free, comprehensive staff
engagement study that will help
you build a winning culture.

TheCultureTool.com